Encounters with God

Encounters with God

Moments that change lives

Peter Hicks

First Published in 2006 by Spring Harvest Publishing Division and
Authentic Media

12 11 10 09 08 07 06   7 6 5 4 3 2 1

Authentic Media
9 Holdom Avenue, Bletchley, Milton Keynes, MK1 1QR, UK
and 129 Mobilization Drive, Waynesboro, GA 30830-4575, USA
www.authenticmedia.co.uk
Authentic Media is a division of Send the Light Ltd., a company
limited by guarantee (registered charity no. 270162)

British Library Cataloguing in Publication Data

A catalogue record for this book is available from
the British Library

ISBN 1-85078-688-7

Cover design by fourninezero.
Print Management by Adare Carwin
Printed in Great Britain by Haynes, Sparkford, Yeovil, Somerset

Contents

Contents

Introduction

This is a book about encountering God.

All through the Bible people encountered God. Or perhaps we ought to say God encountered them. Moses at the mountain, Jonah in the sea, Peter and John by the lake. Because God is very big, much too big to take in at one go, no two encounters were the same. Job met him as the fantastic God who creates monsters and speaks out of the storm. John met him as the one who flooded his life with love. To Hagar he came as the God who cares; to Elijah the God who refreshes.

In this book we look at 30 encounters, covering 30 aspects of our great God. Our aim is not just to study Bible characters or even to build up a clearer understanding of who God is. It is to experience this God for ourselves, the real God, the living God; the God of Abraham and Isaac and Jacob and Samuel and Ezekiel and John and Paul and Jesus himself. Why study God's grace if it doesn't warm our hearts? Why study his glory if it doesn't blow our minds? Why study his holiness if it doesn't make us more like him? Why study God if we don't end up knowing him better?

So this is a book to use as a means of encountering God. For that reason it's probably not wise to read it too fast. The 30 chapters would best be spread over 30 days, with time to meditate and pray over each aspect of God, giving him time to speak and come and work in us. Each chapter ends with a short prayer; to say even those prayers will impact our lives. To take the profound truths revealed by God in each of these encounters and turn them into wholehearted prayer and commitment that God will make them living realities could have the most momentous results.

Sooner or later everyone encounters God. Even those who spend their lives avoiding him will meet him in the end. But why wait? He's the God who comes, who shows his greatness and love and power and goodness. 'Seek my face,' he says. Because everyone who seeks finds.

1.

Moses and the glory of God

'Show me your glory,' said Moses.

He had already seen some of it: a bush blazing with it; a mountain shaking with it. He had watched as God in power and majesty rescued his people from the Egyptians. He had gazed upon it as he talked with God as a man talks with his friend. His face had shone with it.

But he was hooked. What he had experienced made him hungry for more. So he asked for it.

Some people seem to be able to manage without God. Maybe they have never met him; they don't know anything of his goodness; they've tasted nothing of his love; they don't believe in his power; they don't feel any need for him.

Others have met him. They've known the thrill of his joy; they've been confronted with his beauty; their hearts have been warmed by his love; they've fallen before his holiness; they've got excited at his truth. And they want more. They know that what they've tasted is the real thing, even if just a small part of the real thing. Out there is something big. Something that, amazingly, we can know more of. And it's there for the asking. So they ask.

Exodus 33 starts badly. While Moses had been with God on Mount Sinai, the Israelites had made a golden calf. Forgetting that they belonged to God, they had presented sacrifices and worship to the calf, and had worked themselves up into an ungodly orgy of revelry. In response God had said that he would no longer be with them. 'Go on up to the land flowing with milk and honey,' he said. 'But I won't be coming with you; you're a stubborn rebellious people, and I might judge and destroy you on the way.'

But Moses had tasted the presence of God. He knew what it was to have God with him and the prospect of going to the Promised Land without him was unacceptable. 'If you don't come with us,' he said, 'we're not going.'

That warmed God's heart. Of course he wanted to be with Moses. And of course he wanted Moses, and the people with him, to know the reality of his goodness, love and power as they travelled to the Promised Land. 'OK,' he said. 'If you're willing to face the implications of having a holy God living among you, I'll come with you.'

It is at that moment that Moses asks, 'Show me your glory' (Ex. 33:18).

No-one really knows what the glory of God is. It is unique to him. And it's big, very big. So much so that those who have caught a glimpse of it have been overwhelmed by it; some have had to ask God to stop showing it because it was more than they could take. In no way is it the sort of thing we can ever understand, or wrap up into a neat package so we've got it well and truly taped; it is much too big and godlike for that. Even so, since God so longs for us to see his glory, the Bible gives us some clues so that we can begin to grasp what it is like.

- *God's glory is heavy.* The word used in the Old Testament for glory has a strong feel of weight or heaviness about it. It is the opposite of trivial or transient or insignificant. It's big; it's weighty; it presses down on us. It forces us to our knees, down flat on our faces. This is God, the glory of God, and it's very, very big.

- *God's glory is God himself.* Exodus 33 links God's glory closely with his presence. None of God's attributes can be separated from his person: we can't have his love or his truth without having him. Glory especially is inseparable from him. It's the expression of his presence. When God came into his temple, the whole place was filled with his glory. Where God is, there is glory.

- *God's glory is the fullness of his nature.* Another way of thinking of God's glory is to see it as the sum of all his attributes. What happens when we mix together power and wisdom and goodness and truth and grace and holiness and beauty and light and justice and compassion and purity and life...? The answer is glory.

- *God's glory in Jesus.* 'We have seen his glory,' wrote John (Jn. 1:14). It was 'the glory of God in the face of Christ,' said Paul (2 Cor. 4:6). For a few minutes on the Mountain of Transfiguration the glory of God shone out from Jesus. Less obvious, but equally real, those with eyes to see could glimpse the glory of God in a thousand ways in his earthly ministry: in the way he looked, the things he said, how he related, his reactions, when he smiled, his purity, his miraculous power, his grace. Jesus was God with us; where God is present glory shines out.

- *God's glory and us.* Because glory belongs to God, and God is so great, we often find it hard to know how to react when we're confronted with it. We find it fascinating and terrifying, wonderful and awesome. It's beautiful and overwhelming. We are lifted up and carried along by it; it flings us on our faces, it is too much to bear. Psalm 29 likens it to a terrific storm, frightening, destructive, yet thrilling and wonderful. Peter saw it and cried, 'Go away from me, Lord; I am a sinful man!' (Lk. 5:8).

- *God's glory and creation.* In countless ways God's creation expresses God. For those willing to see it, he shows us his glory. In the marvel of the Milky Way, or the beauty of a sunset, or the crash of waves against the cliffs, we catch a glimpse of the glory of the One who made all these things. But only a glimpse; it would be wrong to confuse the glory of created things with the glory of the creator. To stop at the glory of a sunset when we can go on to see the glory of God's face would be like being content with a map of the night sky when we could go out and gaze at the real thing. The Bible tells us that creation itself trembles before God's glory. At the end of the age when the full glory of God is finally revealed the whole earth will shake and begin to disintegrate; the heavenly bodies will be thrown off course. Even before then when 'the glory of the Lord' is revealed, valleys will be raised up, mountains brought low, rough ground smoothed out and rugged places made level (Is. 40:4-5).

- *God's glory and the cross.* Somehow, in a way we struggle to grasp, the greatest moment of glory for Jesus was the cross. 'The hour has come,' he said, 'for the Son of Man to be glorified... my heart is troubled, and

what shall I say? "Father, save me from this hour"?
No, it was for this very reason I came to this hour.
Father, glorify your name!' (Jn. 12:23, 27-28)

What can we do with the glory of God? Most people
miss out on it altogether. Some don't believe in it; even if
God confronts them with it they don't realize what it is.
This can be true even of Christians too. Perhaps their
God is so small that there's no room for anything resem-
bling glory. Sometimes we are afraid that a glorious God
might get up to all sorts of amazing things, and are
determined to remain firmly in control.

Moses was hungry for the glory of God. The more he
tasted it the more he wanted. That's why he cried out to
God to show him his glory. And God did. He put him in
a cleft of a rock and covered him with his hand as his
glory passed by. Then he removed his hand. Just what
Moses saw we are not told. God's glory is such that
words are always inadequate. But God had answered his
prayer (Ex. 33:18-23).

God has many ways of answering a prayer for his
glory. To one person he demonstrates his power by
doing a miracle. For another he thrills their heart with
his presence. One time the demonstration of his glory
will be awesome, even terrifying. Another time it will be
beautiful, breathtaking in its loveliness. Sometimes it
will be personal, just between us and him. Other times
he'll show his glory on a wider canvas, so that any with
eyes to see may recognize it.

That brings us to another point: to pray for God's glory
in the long term is much more than asking for a personal
experience. God doesn't want to share his glory with one
or two. His longing is that 'the earth will be filled with the
knowledge of the glory of the LORD, as the waters cover
the sea' (Hab. 2:14). The glory of so great a God must

blaze out to every corner of his creation. 'Be exalted, O God, above the heavens; let your glory be over all the earth' (Ps. 57:5). 'Show your glory, Lord, in planet earth. Though we've ignored you, and rejected you, treated your world as though it was ours, abused its resources, broken your laws, defiled our minds and our bodies, sinned against those around us, worshipped our golden calves – even here, Lord, show your glory. Even where the darkness is darkest, break through with your light.'

How hungry are you for God's glory? Are you prepared to pray for it, even if God may answer in some way you wouldn't choose? 'Watch out,' said God to his people, 'if I come with you and my glory blazes out and you are unprepared it may consume you.'

Moses' prayer gave him a problem. His face shone. He had been with God, gazing on his glory, and so when people looked at him they saw the light of God's glory reflected there. It was so powerful that people were afraid, so Moses wore a veil, at any rate until the glory faded (Ex. 34:29-35). Paul picks this up in 2 Corinthians 3:7-18. Amazingly, he says that what happened to Moses can happen to every one of us. We too can 'contemplate' or gaze on God's glory, and as we do we'll 'reflect' it (the word he uses in verse 18 means both 'contemplate' and 'reflect').

What is more, that's what our God calls us to do. He doesn't want us to carry on at our ordinary human level. He wants us to get in touch with his glory, to get filled up with it, and then to radiate it to the world around us. No covering up, or hiding under a bucket; instead, the earth is to be filled with the knowledge of the glory of God as it radiates out from us.

Please show me your glory, Lord. I want to see you more clearly, to worship you more worthily, to know the wonder of having so great a God.

2.

The Sons of Korah and the living God

Moses was hungry for the glory of God. Now we come to some guys who were thirsty for the living God.

I guess they were a kind of worship band. They were around for quite a time, new members taking the place of older ones as they got past it. They seemed to have kept the band within the family, all of them looking back to the Levite Korah as their ancestor. And they wrote songs; the lyrics of about a dozen of them have been preserved for us in the book of Psalms. (If you want to find them there's a group from Psalm 42-49, including Psalm 43 which was probably originally joined on to Psalm 42, and then another group from Psalm 84-88, excepting Psalm 86.)

As all good song writers, the Sons of Korah included a range of elements in their songs: worship, prayer, lament, faith, doctrine, joy, sorrow, praise, confidence, questioning and hope. Some of their lyrics are full of celebration and excitement. Some are much more subdued. Like all of us, they went through tough times, when prayers weren't being answered and God seemed far

away. But there's a strong element that runs through
their songs which comes out clearly in Psalm 42:2 and
Psalm 84:2: 'My soul thirsts for God, for the living God',
'...my heart and my flesh cry out for the living God.'
These men believed in God. But their God wasn't any
old god. He was the living God.

Jeremiah was not generally a cheerful character. But
he enjoyed a bit of sarcasm every now and then. 'Look at
the gods of the nations,' he said. 'What a worthless lot
they are. Someone goes and chops down a tree in the forest. Then they cut it to shape and stick gold and silver on
it. To make it stand up they have to nail it into position.'
Jeremiah continues, 'Like a scarecrow in a melon patch,
their idols cannot speak; they must be carried because
they cannot walk. Do not fear them; they can do no harm
nor can they do any good.... But the LORD is the true God;
he is the living God, the eternal King' (Jer. 10:3-10).

The word Jeremiah uses there for 'the LORD' is a word
with a long history. It goes right back to when God met
with Moses at the burning bush, calling him to go and
lead his people out of Egypt. Moses said to God,
'Suppose I go to the Israelites and say to them, "The God
of your fathers has sent me to you," and they ask me,
"What is his name?" Then what shall I tell them?' God
said to Moses, 'I AM WHO I AM. This is what you are to say
to the Israelites: "I AM has sent me to you"' (Ex. 3:13-14).

Moses wasn't just after a new title for God; he was
asking God to unpack who he really was, to give a name
that expressed his nature. In reply God called himself the
I AM, and this is the name that occurs more times than
any other name for God in the Bible. It is traditionally
translated 'the LORD', but since it is based on the Hebrew
word that means 'to be', it could well be translated as
'the One who is.' There may be plenty of gods around,
but all of them except one are empty, hollow, unreal.

Only the I AM is real. Only he is living, pulsating with being. It's only in him that anything can even begin to be. He is the source of all being; everything depends on him for its existence and reality.

God is the living God. When John saw a vision of Jesus as he is now glorified in heaven, he heard him say, 'I am the Living One' (Rev. 1:18). The powers of evil and darkness had done their utmost to destroy the living God, to cast him off the throne of the universe and set themselves there instead. But Easter morning demonstrated with dramatic power that light is stronger than darkness, life has defeated death. Our God is the living God. Jesus is the Risen and Living One; we are a resurrection people.

The best known psalms of the Sons of Korah are brimming over with trust and confidence in this living God. 'God is our refuge and strength,' they say, 'an ever-present help in trouble.' He's 'the LORD Almighty...our fortress'; he is 'God'; he will be 'exalted in the earth' (Ps. 46:1,7,10). He's 'the great King over all the earth'; he 'reigns over the nations'; 'the kings of the earth belong to God; he is greatly exalted' (Ps. 47:2,8,9). He makes his people 'secure for ever'; they drink in his 'unfailing love' and rejoice in his 'righteousness'. 'For this God is our God for ever and ever; he will be our guide even to the end' (Ps. 48:8,9,10,14).

But not all the psalms of the Sons of Korah are like that. That's because they were real people and they lived in the real world. Real people find life tough. God doesn't always scatter our enemies. Goodness doesn't always defeat evil. Prayers aren't always answered the way we want them. Sin and suffering and injustice and evil seem for at least a time to have the upper hand. And sometimes the darkness is so great we can't see any light at all.

The Sons of Korah knew all about that. In the darkest of their psalms they wrote about their soul being full of trouble, their life drawing near to the grave, helpless, powerless.

> You have put me in the lowest pit,
>   in the darkest depths.
> Your wrath lies heavily upon me;
>   you have overwhelmed me with all your waves.
> You have taken from me my closest friends
>   and have made me repulsive to them.
> I am confined and cannot escape;
>   my eyes are dim with grief.
>
> Why, O LORD, do you reject me
>   and hide your face from me?
> From my youth I have been afflicted and close to death;
>   I have suffered your terrors and am in despair.
> Your wrath has swept over me;
>   your terrors have destroyed me.
> All day long they surround me like a flood;
>   they have completely engulfed me.
> You have taken my companions and loved ones from me;
>   the darkness is my closest friend. (Ps. 88:6-9,14-18)

But, for all the darkness and pain, the Sons of Korah are still firm in their trust in God. The whole psalm is addressed to the living God, 'O LORD, the God who saves me' (Ps. 88:1). Grim though life may be, the living God is still there, and we can trust him in his way and his time to save us.

We all know, in theory at any rate, that the reality of God doesn't depend on our circumstances. Joseph may well have felt that God had ceased to exist, or at least deserted him when he was thrown into a pit by his brothers and later thrown into prison by Potiphar. We know the end of the story, and so it is easy for us to see how God was at work even in these apparent disasters. But when disasters happen to us we have no idea how the story is going to end, and so it is much harder to trust.

The Sons of Korah had learned a key lesson about God: he doesn't depend upon us or our circumstances for his reality. When things are great, he's there, working out his purposes; when things are grim, he's still there, working out purposes which as yet we don't understand. Three times in the space of two psalms the Sons of Korah cry, 'Why are you downcast, O my soul? Why so disturbed within me? Put your hope in God, for I will yet praise him, my Saviour and my God' (Ps. 42:5,11; 43:5).

So here are four great principles we can learn from this Old Testament worship band. For each one I've selected a verse or two of their lyrics. If you're good at song writing maybe you could set them to music. But even if you can't, you can still work at singing their God-filled tune with your life.

1. *God's reality doesn't depend on our feelings.* This is the truth we've just been exploring, but it is worth repeating. Our feelings change; one day we're feeling great and God is near. Another day we're really down and God seems a million miles away. But our feelings or circumstances don't change God. He's still the same, real, loving, powerful and living.

> Therefore we will not fear, though the earth give way
> and the mountains fall into the heart of the sea....
> The Lord Almighty is with us;
> the God of Jacob is our fortress. (Ps. 46:2,7)

2. *The living God is for meeting and knowing.* When God
   seems far away we may sometimes be tempted to
   think that we've no option but to settle for a distant
   God. The Sons of Korah refused to do that. They
   knew that there was something far more that God
   wanted them to have. So they cried out for it.

   > As the deer pants for streams of water,
   >   so my soul pants for you, O God.
   > My soul thirsts for God, for the living God.
   >
   > How lovely is your dwelling-place,
   >   O LORD Almighty!
   > My soul yearns, even faints,
   >   for the courts of the LORD;
   > my heart and my flesh cry out
   >   for the living God. (Ps. 42:1-2, 84:1-2)

3. *We must look for him in the right place.* In their songs the
   Sons of Korah are continually expressing their longing to go to the place where they will encounter God.
   They describe this place as the house of God, his holy
   mountain, the place where God dwells, the city of
   God, Mount Zion, the city of the Great King, the temple of God, God's dwelling place, the courts of the
   LORD, God's altar, and the gates of Zion. Several of
   their songs also sing about pilgrimages to the holy
   city and processions up to God's temple. Clearly here
   they're thinking of Jerusalem, the place where God
   had chosen to meet his people. Although God has
   always been free to meet his people anywhere, he has
   chosen certain places where he draws especially near
   to us. One of them is the place of prayer, where we
   spend time seeking his face. Another is the Bible,
   where we hear his voice. A third is the place of

worship along with others, where we know the moving of the Spirit as we praise and wait on him. Then there are the more personal holy places, perhaps somewhere we go on 'retreat', or the company and ministry of a godly friend.

> Blessed are those who dwell in your house;
>   they are ever praising you.
> Blessed are those whose strength is in you,
>   who have set their hearts on pilgrimage.
>
> They go from strength to strength,
>   till each appears before God in Zion.
>
> Better is one day in your courts
>   than a thousand elsewhere;
> I would rather be a doorkeeper in the house of my God
>   than dwell in the tents of the wicked. (Ps. 84:4-5,7,10)

4. *The living God is for celebrating.* Of course there are times when the last thing we want to do is celebrate anything. But the living God still deserves to be celebrated. It may well be that making the effort to lift up our eyes from our problems and pains and to focus them on him will do us good. It seems pretty clear that the Sons of Korah, whatever their personal circumstances, had great fun as they led the triumphant worship of God's people, maybe even dancing through the streets of Jerusalem as they declared God's greatness.

> Clap your hands, all you nations;
>   shout to God with cries of joy.
> How awesome is the LORD Most High,
>   the great King over all the earth!

> Sing praises to God, sing praises;
>> sing praises to our King, sing praises.
>
> For God is King of all the earth;
>> sing to him a psalm of praise. (Ps. 47:1-2,6-7)
>
> Great is the LORD, and most worthy of praise,
>> in the city of our God, his holy mountain.
> For this God is our God for ever and ever;
>> he will be our guide even to the end. (Ps. 48:1,14)

That's your God. Real, dynamic, awesome, living. Are you thirsty for him? Or have you settled for a dull, useless sort of god? Have you let your feelings shape your faith? Or are you determined, like the Sons of Korah, to go for the real thing?

> *Yes, Lord, I want the real thing. I want you, the living God. Forgive me that so often my religion has been dominated by me, my feelings and my situation. From now on, Lord, may it be dominated by you, the living God.*

3.

Paul and the life-giving God

Moses hungered for the glory of God. The Sons of Korah thirsted for the living God. Paul was willing to give up everything – position, status, reputation, possessions, even life itself – in order to know God in Christ.

> I consider everything a loss compared to the surpassing greatness of knowing Christ Jesus my Lord, for whose sake I have lost all things. I consider them rubbish, that I may gain Christ and be found in him, not having a righteousness of my own that comes from the law, but that which is through faith in Christ – the righteousness that comes from God and is by faith. I want to know Christ and the power of his resurrection and the fellowship of sharing in his sufferings, becoming like him in his death, and so, somehow, to attain to the resurrection from the dead.
>
> Not that I have already obtained all this, or have already been made perfect, but I press on to take hold of that for which Christ Jesus took hold of me. Brothers, I do not consider myself yet to have taken hold of it. But one thing I do: Forgetting what is behind and straining towards what is ahead, I press on towards the goal to win the prize for which God has called me heavenwards in Christ Jesus. (Phil. 3:8-14)

Paul had pondered deeply on the mysteries of God's ways, and was convinced that the key to the heart and purposes of God lay in the death and resurrection of Jesus. It is here that we find him at his most godlike; it was here that Paul wanted to 'know' him, to draw near to his heart, to receive his grace, to plumb the depths of his salvation, to meet him face to face. As he expresses in this passage his deep hunger and thirst for God we can pick out seven great truths for our own lives about our relationship with this life-giving God.

* *God has given his life for us.* There's a price that had to be paid to redeem a lost world, and to break the hold of sin and evil on our lives. In his early years Paul had sincerely believed that human effort was good enough to set everything right, but later he realized that this could never be so (Phil. 3:6,9). Only God could do what was needed, and that at great cost to himself. For years Paul had thought he knew all about the Jewish sacrifices, how animals and birds had to forfeit their lives so that God's people could find forgiveness and salvation. But only when he came face to face with the reality of Jesus' death did he realize what they meant. All those animals pouring out their lives were pictures, pointers to the one great sacrifice, the only one that was effective: the pouring out of the life of God on the cross of Calvary. God has given his life for us. The living God valued us so highly that he gave his very being – his life – to break the hold of evil and make us his.

* *God gives his life to us.* Not only has God given his life for us; now in his grace and resurrection power he gives his life to us. Like the Sons of Korah, Paul knew that God was the living God. All his life he thirsted

for him. When he became a Christian he realized that instead of us winning God's favour as he had been trying to do, the living God comes to us and puts his life in us. It is not we who live, but God in Christ who lives in us. Here's the amazing purpose of God, that he should live in us, and that we should know his life. 'Because I live, you also will live,' said Jesus. 'If anyone loves me, he will obey my teaching. My Father will love him, and we will come to him and make our home with him'. 'Remain in me, and I will remain in you' (Jn. 14:19,23, 15:4).

- *This life-giving God is ours to know.* When the Bible talks about knowing God it means something far richer than knowing *about* God. True, it is our privilege to come to know many rich truths about him and his nature and his ways; the Bible is packed with them, and the more we get to know the more there is yet to learn. But to know God merely on this level is hopelessly inadequate – even the devil knows lots about God. When the Bible talks about knowing God its key thrust is knowing God personally, having a personal relationship with him. Personal relationships are close and intimate. They are life-sharing. A personal relationship with God means that as he shares his life with me, I share my life with him. They are also life-changing. If I know something, says the Bible, it must affect my actions. To know God means that my life is shaped and changed by him. 'I want to know Christ,' wrote Paul, 'I long for a deep life sharing, life-changing relationship with him.'

- *There's always more.* When Paul wrote to the Philippians he already knew Christ, probably better than any of us could claim. But he was only too aware that there was so much more to know. 'I haven't arrived,' he says. 'There's still a long way to go. But I'm determined to go forward. This is what it's all about. This is why God has called me heavenwards in Christ Jesus. And nothing's going to stop me.' The problem with many of us is that we've got stuck. We know God a bit. Perhaps we know God better than others. So we are satisfied; we think that's enough. Why go to the trouble of getting to know him better when we can get by on what we've got? The Bible's answer is clear. There's so much more. God didn't pour out his life so that we could have a superficial relationship with him, knowing only something of his love and power and goodness. He gave everything so that we might have everything.

- *The life of God in us is the answer to all sorts of things.* For years Paul struggled with the issue of righteousness. He was driven by a desire to be right with God and righteous in every part of his living. But he was constantly dogged by failure; however hard he tried righteousness eluded him – until God in Christ came with his life-giving power and lived in him. True, it didn't make him perfect overnight; but it solved the problem. Righteousness comes from God; in faith we receive it when God comes to live in us (Phil. 3:9). And it is the same with so many other things. What is the secret of power? How do we receive guidance? How can we live a holy life? How do we bring others to Jesus? How do we cope with setbacks and suffering? How do we change the world? The answer to all these is the life of God in us.

- *God's life is inseparable from Christ's suffering and death.* Verse 10 rightly starts by stating that to know Christ is to know the power of his resurrection; to have the living God in us means we experience the tremendous power of that life, as seen in the resurrection of Christ. But then it goes on to speak of suffering and death; indeed Paul seems as keen to experience these as he is to experience resurrection power. This brings us to a profound point which we often miss. If God in Christ lives in me, then, certainly, the power of his life will live in me. But, equally, since the world rejects God and doesn't want anything to do with him, I'll get from those around me all the rejection and opposition it feels towards him. 'If we belonged to the world' said Jesus, 'it would love us as its own.' But we don't, so it hates us, as it hated him. It persecuted him, and so it will persecute us (Jn. 15:18-20). 'They will treat you this way because of my name, for they do not know the One who sent me' (Jn. 15:21). Nor is it just those around us who will be opposed to God's life in us; the devil and all his dark powers will do their utmost to break us and thwart the purposes of God in and through our lives. If Christ suffered and was crucified, we can expect no less. Instead of running from such suffering, Paul almost welcomed it since it was an evidence of the reality of God's life in him.

- *If you get anything, get the life of God in you.* 'It may mean suffering and death' says Paul, 'but it's worth it. It may mean sacrifice, but what is a sacrifice when God gives everything? Compared with this nothing is of any value. Whatever it costs; whatever obstacles may be in the way; however attractive alternatives may seem – make the life of God in you your priority' (see Phil. 3:7-8,13-14).

If you're anything like me you will have often felt that your spiritual experience falls far behind Paul's. So if even he was hungry for more of the life-giving God, then surely we should be too. Through the cross and the resurrection God has made it possible for us to know him, to experience his life in us and all that that means. Settle it in your mind now that you're not going to be content with anything less; then confirm your decision with God by turning Philippians 3:8-14 into your own personal prayer.

4.

Open-hearted disciples and the life-changing God

Everyone has a chance to meet the living God – probably many chances. In all sorts of ways God comes near, calls, speaks. Even atheists experience it. Something stirs inside them; a door begins to open; a seedling thought comes into their mind. And they have a choice. To take notice, push on the door, hear the voice. Or to reject it, to slam the door shut again.

God walked in the garden in the cool of the day, and the man and the woman hid themselves (Gen. 3:8). God called to Moses from within the bush, and Moses said, 'Here I am' (Ex. 3:4). Jesus said to the rich young man, 'Sell your possessions and give to the poor. Then come, follow me.' And the man went away sad (Mt. 19:21). 'Follow me,' he said to Levi. At once he left everything and followed him.

'All day long' said God, 'I held out my hands to a disobedient and obstinate people' (Rom. 10:21). To the people of pagan Nineveh he sent Jonah the prophet, and they listened and turned from their evil ways (Jon. 3:3-10). To Athens he sent Paul; some sneered; but others said, 'We want to hear you again on this subject' (Acts 17:32). To a friend of mine he spoke when the bottom dropped out his world; to another when she met a true Christian; to another when he held his newborn child in his arms. Each had a choice, to listen or to turn away.

John sums up the ministry of Jesus: 'The true light that gives light to every man was coming into the world. He was in the world, and though the world was made through him, the world did not recognize him. He came to that which was his own, but his own did not receive him. Yet to all who received him, to those who believed in his name, he gave the right to become the children of God' (Jn. 1:9-12).

When God comes we can open our lives and hearts to him. Or we can shut them. In John's experience most shut. But some opened. And the results were life-changing. To those who did receive him he gave something incredible: the gift of becoming children of God. Years before on the lakeside four fishermen had heard the words, 'Follow me, and I will make you fishers of men.' At the time they hadn't realized all that they meant. But they followed, and Jesus changed their lives.

Of course it makes sense. Put a lion in a henhouse, and something's going to happen. Sit on an erupting volcano, and you won't sit for long. Put the life of the living God inside me, and it is bound to make a difference. The life of God isn't something little and insignificant that I can have without noticing it. It's big. It's got to be life-changing.

From the first moment those disciples started following Jesus their lives started to change. But they didn't become sinless children of God or expert fishers of men overnight.

God could change our lives immediately if he chose. But I guess the shock would be too much for us. Instead he starts a process. Each process is tailor-made to the individual. He knows what we need, where we need to change, what the priorities are. He knows how to change us – gently or more radically, by a miracle or through hard work, whether to start with our beliefs or our feelings. He knows where old hurts need healing, old ideas sorting out, old sins dealing with. He knows the hidden parts of our lives that we're not even aware of, things that motivate us or hold us in bondage, secret wounds, fears and feelings that lie deep inside us. He knows when to tackle them, and how to transform them.

He's the master potter, taking the broken vase and remoulding it into something beautiful and new. His programme of change is comprehensive. It covers our values, our ambitions, our relationships, our possessions, our past, our goals, our attitudes, our weaknesses, our thoughts, our motivation, our strong points, our blind spots, our work, our beliefs, our actions, our emotions, our reactions, our being, our future. Put the life of God in me and sooner or later every bit of me will be affected, like yeast working its way through a lump of dough.

There's something special about God's life-changing power. It has the power to do the impossible. In my garden is a dead plum tree. Not far away is a living one. If I took a branch of the living tree and stuck it into the dead one, there's no way the dead one would come alive. Instead the living branch would die. If I put a rotten apple into a box of good apples, the whole box will go rotten; in no way would putting a good apple into a box of rotten apples make the whole box good. But God does that with us; his life changes our deadness to life, our badness to good.

Ezekiel described a valley full of dry bones. That's where God has to start. Not just problem people, but dead people. Not just corpses, but bones. Not just skeletons but broken and scattered bones. But even that was not a problem to the life-giving power of God. Into those bones came his amazing life, and, says Ezekiel, 'they came to life and stood up on their feet – a vast army' (Ezek. 37:10).

There's nothing in us that is too hard for God to change, no part of us where his life can't get to work. 'Impossible' doesn't appear in his vocabulary. He can make fishermen into apostles. He can turn prejudice into love. He can make strengths out of weaknesses. He can shape saints out of sinners. The only thing that can stop his life-changing power working its way through every bit of my life is my refusal to let it happen.

God's vision is to make us like him. My daughter is like me (in some ways!) because she has some of my life in her. An acorn produces an oak tree because it has oak life in it. Set God's life to work in me, and I will become godlike. Holy, true, pure, loving, gracious, filled with the fruit of God's Spirit, like Jesus. 'Children of God,' said John, 'born of God' (Jn. 1:12-13), with the life of God pulsing in their veins enabling and empowering and continuing to shape them into their Father's likeness.

Acorns take time to grow into oak trees. God took time over those early disciples. Some things changed pretty quickly: the direction of their lives, for example. Other things took longer; ingrained beliefs took years to eradicate. Four years after he had first met Jesus, Peter was still struggling with racial prejudice. But God worked steadily on. 'Now we are children of God,' wrote John, towards the end of his life; 'what we will be has not yet been made known. But we know that when he appears, we shall be like him, for we shall see him as he is. Everyone who has this hope in him purifies himself, just as he is pure' (1 Jn. 3:2-3). Many of us feel we are just beginning on the process of becoming like Jesus. All of us know we've still a long way to go. But the key to progress is willingness to let his life-changing power work in us.

How willing are you to let God's life change your life? How much freedom are you willing to let him have to make you into what he wants you to be? How about working through these nine steps, inviting, or re-inviting him to fill you with his life?

1. *Open the front door.* 'I'm there knocking' he says. 'I'm the Living One, and I want to come into your life. I want to transform your life, to make it what I intended it to be. You have the choice, to keep me outside, or to let me in.'

2. *Invite him in.* Don't expect him to slip in unnoticed. Make something of it. Give him a warm welcome. Make it big; make it real. 'Come on, God, the living God, the amazing God, the holy God, the God of glory. Come right in, now, my Lord and my God.'

3. *Hand over the keys.* This may take some doing. It's one thing to invite him into the front room. It's quite another to give him the keys to the shed at the bottom of the garden, or to the things we've stored in the loft, or kept hidden away under the bed. But if his life is going to permeate your life, you've got to give him the keys to each part. When he uses them to unlock the various areas is up to him. For a time he may concentrate on sorting out your anger or the TV programmes you watch, leaving those deep seated hurts from the past and your fear of thunderstorms for later. But you need to give him the keys now.

4. *Give him the colour chart.* He's into transforming, so he needs to choose the colour of the new paint. He won't

just put it on without checking with you, but he expects you to give him the go ahead. A good coat of love – probably several coats to make sure. And then a pot or two of joy. And then a wall of peace. And a covering of patience. And somewhere a coat of kindness, and goodness, and faithfulness, and gentleness and self-control. Lots of good colours, all over the place, glowing with the character of Jesus, radiant with his life.

5. *Put up with demolition.* Most builders would do the demolishing before the painting, but God doesn't necessarily work that way. He doesn't want to demolish everything; there are things he's content to change gradually. But sometimes there's a wall or even a whole room of our lives that needs demolishing. Demolition is a messy job; it stirs up lots of dirt. When God does it to part of our lives it's likely to hurt. A relationship that has to end. Indulgence in sin that has to stop. An idol that has to be thrown down.

6. *Take up tools.* Of course he's in charge; but when you see what colour he's planned for the living area, pick up a scraper or a brush and give him a hand. Maybe he's chosen a soft shade of peace. So get alongside him and scrape away at worry and stress and anxiety. Try out some trust; work at remembering that you have a Heavenly Father who's committed to caring for you. Get hold of a brush and cover your thoughts and reactions with a good coating of his peace.

7. *Give way.* 'But God, I don't like the colour you've chosen. And the demolition is hurting too much. If I'd known you were going to do it that way, I wouldn't have asked you in in the first place.' 'But you did ask me in. And this way is my way. I know you find it

hard; I know it hurts. But don't you trust me? I know the beautiful thing I'm going to make out of your life; and this is the way to do it. Do you really want to miss out on everything, just because this hurts?'

8. *Be patient.* We would choose the short cuts, the easy way to Christlikeness. But Jesus didn't choose that for his early disciples; he took years to shape them. For the most part he doesn't do it with us, either. So, again, we have to learn to trust what he's doing and the way he's doing it.

9. *But be impatient too!* Don't let a patient trust that accepts God's methods and programme make you smug and self-satisfied. 'Yes, I know I've got a problem with porn, but God hasn't got round to delivering me from it yet, so I'll carry on.' No way! He may take time to undo the damage sin has done, and a long time to break its hold on your mind. But what he expects from us is a holy dissatisfaction with all that's still wrong with our lives, and urgent prayer to him to push forward with the process of making us like him.

Revelation 3:20 is one of the best-known verses in the Bible. In it Jesus spoke to the half-hearted Christians of Laodicea and asked them to open the door and let him in. He's saying the same to you today. Yours is the choice to say yes or no. If you say 'yes' you can be absolutely certain of one thing: he will keep his promise: 'I will come in.'

It is so amazing, Lord of glory, that you want to live in my life. What else can I say, but 'Come in'? I open the door; live in me; get to work on every part of me; be my life-changing God.

5.

Job and the fantastic God

Once upon a time there were four wise men. They weren't wise in just one or two areas, like most clever people today. They were wise in every area you could be wise in. They knew all there was to know. They were experts in philosophy, science, ethics, and especially in theology. What's more, they were all very wealthy, because, as everybody knows, if you are clever you do well and make lots of money and everything in life is great. And they were nice guys, well-behaved, respected in the community, thoughtful and kind, ready to help anyone in trouble. All the people around, who were nowhere near so wise or so wealthy, turned to them whenever they had any problems, and listened to their advice, and benefited from their wisdom. The four wise men were good friends and got together every so often to discuss wise things together.

There was also a fifth man, who was wise, but not as wise as the four wise men. That was because he was young, and in those days it wasn't possible to be young and ever so wise at the same time. One of the results of being young, and so one of the reasons why he wasn't ever so wise, was that he felt strongly about things;

indeed, certain things made him angry. So he was an angry-young-not-ever-so-wise man.

The wisest of the four wise men was called Job. Not only was he very wise, he was also really religious and very good. And God was very pleased with him; in fact, he was quite proud of him.

One day the unthinkable happened. At four fell swoops Job lost everything he had, except his wife. Oxen, donkeys, servants, sheep, camels, sons and daughters – the lot. Shattered and broken, Job tore his robe and shaved his head. Then he fell before God and said: 'Naked I came from my mother's womb, and naked I shall depart. The LORD gave and the LORD has taken away; may the name of the LORD be praised' (Job 1:21).

As though that wasn't enough, a few days later two more disasters struck. Horrible sores erupted all over Job's body. As he sat on the ash heap scraping at the sores with a bit of broken pot, his wife, the only thing he had left, started telling him to end it all, to curse God and die.

When the news reached the other three wise men they met together and set out to see Job. Even before they got to him, they were overwhelmed by the extent of his disasters. They hardly recognized him, and when they came near they wept and tore their robes. Then, like true friends and wise men, they sat on the ground with him for seven days and seven nights in total silence (Job 2:11-13).

At the end of that time, in horror at himself and at all that had happened, Job cursed the day that he was born.

'May the day of my birth perish,
   and the night it was said, "A boy is born!"
That day – may it turn to darkness;
   may God above not care about it.

'That night – may thick darkness seize it;
    may it not be included among the days of the year.

'Why did I not perish at birth,
    and die as I came from the womb?
For now I would be lying down in peace;
    I would be asleep and at rest.' (Job 3:3-4,6,11,13)

Then it started. After all, they were wise men. They were
the experts. They knew all the answers. So off they went
on a long debate. What's going on here? Why the disasters? What's God up to? What does it mean? Why
should a good man suffer? They didn't all agree, though
most of what they said was pretty wise. But not much of
it did Job any good. He let them talk, listened to their
arguments, raised his objections, and again and again
cried out in pain of body and soul and in protest to God
who was seemingly oblivious to what he was going
through.

After nearly thirty chapters the angry young man,
who had waited impatiently because he knew that you
should always be silent before your elders and wisers,
could stand it no more. He burst out with his anger and
his answer – a pretty good one, in the circumstances.

And that's it. All the wisest men of the day, plus a
good dose of youthful passion, explaining the deep mysteries of human existence, of life and death and suffering; mapping the ways of God, and solving the problems
of the world.

Then God speaks. He doesn't contradict what all the
wise men have said, though his first comment puts the
wisest and best of them firmly in place: 'Who is this that
darkens my counsel [or questions my purposes] with
words without knowledge?' (Job 38:2). What he does is
simply to state clearly and strongly that he is God, and

he knows what he is doing. The wisest of human beings is not God, and does not know what God is doing.

Four chapters later God waits for Job's reply.

Then Job replied to the LORD:

'I know that you can do all things;
    no plan of yours can be thwarted.
You asked, "Who is this that obscures my counsel without
    knowledge?"
    Surely I spoke of things I did not understand,
    things too wonderful for me to know.

'You said, "Listen now, and I will speak;
    I will question you,
    and you shall answer me."
My ears had heard of you
    but now my eyes have seen you.
Therefore I despise myself
    and repent in dust and ashes.' (Job 42:1-6)

People puzzle over what's happening here. All through the book Job has been protesting his innocence and the unfairness of God in allowing him to suffer; all through the book all five men have been struggling with the question, 'Why?' To many it seems profoundly unsatisfactory that at the last Job gives way and accepts that he is wrong to demand an answer. But we need to remember two things.

The first is that the book of Job does not say there is no answer. In fact it gives us a glimpse into part of the answer by describing the activities of Satan and of God behind the scenes in chapters 1 and 2. There most definitely is a reason why God allows Job to suffer; what's more God knows the end of the story, related in the last verses of chapter 42, when he brings good out of all the evil.

The second thing we need to remember is the hint given in Job's words, 'My ears had heard of you but now my eyes have seen you.' There's all the difference in the world between knowing lots of theology – not to mention philosophy, ethics and science – and meeting the real, living, glorious God. When we're operating on the level of theory or reason or logic we can question and debate and protest; when we're confronted with the greatness of the Sovereign Lord of the universe, we realize how utterly inadequate all our ideas and arguments are.

Spurred on by the pain and injustice of it all, eloquent in his arguments, Job had cried out to God to answer his case. God doesn't brush Job's cries aside. But the heart of his response is not, 'Listen to my reply to the issues raised by the debate,' but 'Look at me. See who I am. Be still and know that I am God. Gaze on me and grasp more clearly what that means.'

When I was a child there were many things I didn't understand. My dad was very wise, so most times he would be able to explain the things that puzzled me. But there were some things that were beyond him, so I stored up a list of the really difficult issues with the intention, 'When I get to heaven I'll ask God.' But I don't think I will. When I get to heaven and see God I won't need to ask him anything. Because when I see him I shall see everything.

It's not so much that the issues will become insignificant, though in some sense that may be so. Rather, in seeing God I shall see the whole: the wisdom, the power, the love, the goodness, the truth that makes sense of everything and puts everything in its right place. In no way did God say to Job, 'Your sufferings are insignificant compared to my great eternal purposes.' In compassion and grace he let Job see at least some of his greatness and glory so that he could see himself and his sufferings in the light of them.

The book of Job, and especially God's words to Job in chapters 38-41, makes great reading. Someone has described the book as one of the greatest poems of all time. But the book and the words of God aren't there just as poetry. The key to the book is that Job comes face to face with the fantastic God. And the book's included in your Bible to bring you face to face with the fantastic God as well.

Why don't you let it do that now? As you read the rest of this chapter, let the Holy Spirit take away any barriers or blockages, so that through him you can truly meet your fantastic God.

- *The fantastic God who cares for you.* Since we assume that God's chief job is to make life as pleasant as possible, when disaster strikes we tend to conclude that God doesn't love us any more. The book of Job makes it clear that this is wrong. God's wise and gracious love for Job didn't waver from chapter 1 to chapter 42.

- *The fantastic God who trusts you.* 'Take away everything Job has' sneered Satan to God, 'and he'll curse you to your face.' But God trusted Job. Job could have blown it; Satan was sure he would. But God knew his man, and trusted him to show that his commitment to God wasn't just for what he could get out of it; it was a commitment to God, not to camels and donkeys and even sons and daughters. I find that awesome, that setbacks and suffering are evidence of my God's trust in me.

- *The fantastic God who is proud of you.* Well, that's how it reads. God really shows off Job to Satan (Job 1:8).

So if you're anywhere near the 'Job league' God will be pretty proud of you too. I fancy that even if you're not, he's still proud of you. I held my nephew's newborn son the other day. He was a good-looking baby and his dad was really proud of him. But I've seen real bashed about patchy faced newborn babies that few would call beautiful – and still their parents are wildly proud of them. Fantastically, your Heavenly Father is wildly proud of you, his child, however spotty your face or weak your Christian life.

- *The fantastic God who created you and your universe.* At the root of my nephew's pride in his son was the fact that in a sense he was his creation; our God allows us to share the terrific privilege of bringing into being another person. All through the book of Job, and especially when God is speaking to Job in chapters 38-41, we read of a God who sovereignly brings into being everything that exists. There's no place for a chance, meaningless universe here. What is, is because of God. The answer to 'Why?' is always ultimately God. That applies to you, to the thunderstorm, to the crocodile, to everything around you, and to all that happens to you.

- *The fantastic God who is Lord of all.* Not only does God bring everything that is into being; he directs the way things work out. As Paul puts it, 'in all things God works for the good of those who love him' (Rom. 8:28). We may have problems with this, wondering how God can fit together all the details of his vast universe without taking away our human freedom. But these are not problems to our fantastic God. He's big enough and clever enough to direct the orbit of a distant star and the fall of a snowflake; his wisdom is deep enough to cope with every one of our free actions and choices, and to fit them into his sovereign purposes. He's so brilliant that he can even use the plots of Satan and the ravages of the powers of evil, turning them on their head to bring about his beautiful purposes, as in the story of Joseph (Gen. 50:20) or on the cross.

- *The fantastic God who does crazy things.* There's something in us that wants God to be well-behaved, orderly and predictable. We like to be able to understand what he's doing and why he's doing it. The book of Job leaves us in no doubt that the real God isn't like that at all. So far from being tame and well-behaved, he's terrifyingly unpredictable. He didn't just create butterflies and primroses; he made behemoth and leviathan (Job 40:15-41:34). I've no idea what behemoth and leviathan are – but God had great fun making them and loves to see them lying under the lotus plants or breathing fire and smoke. I've no idea why God created such a vast universe, galaxy upon galaxy, or such tiny sub-nuclear particles, billions of them in a grain of sand. Why does he make black holes and supernovas? Why does he fill distant planets with breathtaking beauty, where nobody will ever see it? Of course, he knows the answers to these questions; but we don't. To us they seem crazy – but that's our fantastic God.

- *The fantastic God whose wisdom and power never fail.* In our frustration, we often try and tell God that our way of doing things would be better; in our darkness we begin to think that he's as helpless as we are. But we're always wrong. His wisdom and power are big, very big, and they never fail.

- *The fantastic God whom you can trust.* Even in the darkness. Even in the pain. Even in the frustration. Because he's your God, and he's fantastic.

  I love you, Lord. I marvel that you're so big, so unpredictable, so fantastic. Life with you can never be dull. Go on, Lord; do your amazing things in my life and in our world. For you are God, the fantastic God.

6.

Israel and the mysterious God

'It's straightforward, really. God loves me. God is all powerful. Since he loves me he'll stop anything nasty happening to me. Since he's all powerful he's got what it takes to make my life wonderful. So being a Christian means that life's going to be absolutely wonderful.'

That's the way the people of God in the Old Testament thought. After all, they were God's chosen people. And he had made all sorts of promises: a land flowing with milk and honey, victory over enemies, lots and lots of blessings. So life was set to be great.

But it didn't work out that way. Nasties happened. Enemies won. Blessings were thin on the ground. And it wasn't just because God's people were disobedient and sinful. As we've seen with Job, bad things happened to good people. One of the most moving passages in the whole of the Old Testament is in Jeremiah 20, where Jeremiah, who, like Job, had faithfully obeyed and followed God even at great cost to himself, cried out in pain and frustration at the way God was doing things.

> O LORD, you deceived me, and I was deceived;
>   you overpowered me and prevailed.

I am ridiculed all day long;
   everyone mocks me.
Whenever I speak, I cry out
   proclaiming violence and destruction.
So the word of the LORD has brought me
   insult and reproach all day long.

Why did I ever come out of the womb
   to see trouble and sorrow
   and to end my days in shame? (Jer. 20:7-8,18)

Those that have studied these things tell us that Jeremiah's tormented cry is not just as a record of how Jeremiah felt, but an expression of the feelings of the whole of Israel. 'So' they cried, 'we're supposed to be the people of God, his treasured possession? Specially loved and protected and empowered and blessed? Where then are the rivers of milk and honey? Where are the cringing enemies? Where's the great life? Where's the fulfilment of all those promises of blessing? What on earth is God up to?'

In the greatest letter he ever wrote Paul spent three chapters struggling with the mystery of God's ways with Israel (Rom. 9-11). Most of us who have studied those chapters come away feeling that though Paul has managed to explain some of the reasons for the way God has worked things out so far, and given us a vision of what he plans to do in the future, the picture is still far from complete. As God himself said to his people,

'...my thoughts are not your thoughts,
   neither are your ways my ways.
As the heavens are higher than the earth,
   so are my ways higher than your ways
   and my thoughts than your thoughts.' (Is. 55:8,9)

God is certainly working out his purposes for Israel, as he was for Job and Jeremiah, and as he is for each one of us. But though we may be able to see more of the picture than Job or Jeremiah did when in the midst of things, we still can't see the whole picture; we don't know what God is up to.

But that's no more than you would expect. After all, God is God. He's big. He doesn't just operate in my little patch. His patch is the whole universe, and beyond. His plans and purposes are big: far, far bigger than my ideas. Even though he's chosen to tell us some profound truths about himself and his ways, he's under no obligation to explain everything to us in fine detail. Indeed, that would be impossible. There's no way my understanding could grasp the hugely complex plans and purposes of so great a God. Of course his thoughts are higher than my thoughts. I can only think according to my incredibly narrow perspective; I can only see a tiny bit of the big picture.

I like to work things out. I like to be able to wrap my mind around things, to crack the problems, to solve the mysteries. That's OK if I'm dealing with things roughly my own size, or the size that my understanding can cope with. But some things are too big for me. I still struggle, for instance, with the truth that time passes at a different rate according to the speed at which you are moving. Maybe one day I will be able to wrap my mind round that one; but what I mustn't do is refuse to believe it, simply because I can't understand it.

That's a mistake some people make about God. They read about God being eternal – without beginning or end – or about the trinity – both three and one. And they can't understand; they can't conceive of something that is without beginning and end, or that is both one and many. So they decide that it cannot be. Or they struggle to reconcile our freedom with God's sovereignty, or the suffering we face with God's love. And because they can't work it all out, they conclude that God doesn't exist. But of course there are things about God that we don't understand. Of course he allows things to happen that we, in our limited way of seeing things, think are a mistake. What else would you expect when you're dealing with so big a God?

Paul ends up his discussion of the mystery of God's purposes for Israel with one of the greatest passages in the whole of the Bible:

> Oh, the depth of the riches of the wisdom and knowledge of God!
>> How unsearchable his judgments.
>> and his paths beyond tracing out!
> 'Who has known the mind of the Lord?
>> Or who has been his counsellor?'
> 'Who has ever given to God,
>> that God should repay him?'
> For from him and through him and to him are all things.
>> To him be the glory for ever! Amen. (Rom. 11:33-36)

Of course we don't understand him! But what would be the point of a god so small we could wrap him up with our poor little minds? Our God is big. Depth and riches of wisdom and knowledge! Cleverer by far than the wisest philosopher or most complex computer. Bigger by far than the biggest thing we could ever imagine. Working out purposes that are hugely complex yet stunningly beautiful. Taking into consideration factors we have never dreamt of. Full of ideas that are stunning in their breadth and daring.

And doing it all in such a godlike way! Not struggling with the issues. Not having to check with us whether or not he's got it right. Not hesitant, unsure, chopping and changing when things catch him off guard. But steadily, gloriously, wonderfully working out his purposes of truth, love, grace and goodness, working all things together, on the great stage of the universe and in the tiniest detail; making sure that his kingdom is coming, his will is being done on earth, and throughout the whole of his incredibly great creation.

'For from him and through him and to him are all things.' Now, there's a truth to marvel at. The tiniest snowflake: from him, through him, to him. The Milky Way: from him, through him, to him. You and me: from him, through him, to him. My life and circumstances: from him, through him, to him. Even the things I don't or don't want to understand: from him, through him, to him. And though we don't see it yet, out of it all will come his perfect and beautiful and amazing fulfilment of all his purposes, and we, with the whole of creation, will see it and marvel, and give him the glory for ever.

Are you into mysteries? Murder mysteries? Detective stories? UFOs? Scientific conundrums? Whatever you're into, don't miss out on the mystery of our God. Leave a tame, dull, wimpish God for others to be bored with. Instead, catch a glimpse of the real God, big, glorious, and profoundly mysterious. Wonder and worship. Stop skating over the surface, spending all your time with trivialities. Go deep. Spend time in awe and wonder. Fall before him and worship. Be overwhelmed by the mystery of your God.

- *The mystery of his immensity.* 'Your God is too small,' wrote J.B. Phillips in the middle of last century. He's right. God's got to be bigger than any concept we may have. So keep growing your ideas about him, 'magnifying the Lord.' Gaze at the Milky Way and remember that that, in all its breathtaking vastness, is just one of the millions of galaxies that God's hands have flung into space. Read the amazing discoveries of the scientists, the complexity of DNA or atomic particles or black holes, and remember that these discoveries are only beginning to scratch the surface of what the things that God has made are really like.

- *The mystery of his nature.* Yes, in his grace he's revealed a lot of truth about himself to us, especially in Jesus. But don't for one moment imagine that he's told us everything. Apart from anything else, there's so much about him that our limited minds could never take on board. And there are plenty of things he's keeping up his sleeve. Even when we get to heaven there'll still be plenty of surprises and loads more to learn and marvel at. 'When we've been there ten thousand years,' there'll still be amazing depths to plumb and heights to scale.

- *The mystery of his ways.* Of course we question. Like Job and Jeremiah and the people of Israel we fail to understand what God is up to; we're sure we can think of a better way of doing things; we're disappointed and frustrated that his ways aren't the same as our ways; we struggle and suffer, and we wonder if we'll make it through. But even though it's hard, we need to hang on with Job, who refused to give up his trust in God, and with Jeremiah, who in the middle of his darkest doubts was able to say, 'But the LORD is with me like a mighty warrior.... He rescues the life of the needy from the hands of the wicked' (Jer. 20:11,13). Whatever we go through, Romans 8:28 stands true: '…in all things God works for the good of those who love him, who have been called according to his purpose.'

- *The mystery of his purposes.* 'Where is he going?' we wonder. 'Why is he doing this? Why has he allowed that to happen?' The answer is that behind it all are the unfathomable and yet perfect purposes of God – for us personally, and for a world and a universe. Despite the teaching of so many around us, nothing is meaningless, nothing is by chance; everything fits into his purposes. Some of the elements of his purposes we know: to redeem and transform a fallen world, to make each one of us like Jesus. But there's so much we don't know. That is why we have to pray, 'Your kingdom come, your will be done.'

- *The mysteries of his love.* 'How can a God of love allow this to happen?' Yesterday I was at the funeral of a close family member who struggled and lost her battle against cancer. I have wept over the death of my baby son, David. I've walked with others through times of deep disappointment and hurt. Do these things show that God's love has worn thin or gone on holiday? I am convinced they do not; indeed, since everything that God does is done in love, I have to accept that even these things, in a way that at the moment is mysterious to me, are expressions of his love. On the smaller scale, of course, I can understand it: it is in love that the parent refuses to let the child indulge in an unhealthy diet, or run freely out on to the main road. Maybe these things can help to give some insight into what our loving Heavenly Father is doing, even though as yet much of his love remains deeply mysterious.

- *The mysteries of his wisdom.* 'Oh, the depth of the riches of the wisdom and knowledge of God!' cried Paul. I love that. Deep and rich. Not just cleverness, but profound and glorious wisdom. Beautiful, rich in colours, amazing in complexity, yet ultimately so simple, so clear, so all-embracing. What to us is darkness, to him is light. What to us is mystery, to him is radiant clarity. He knows; he understands. Thank goodness there's something bigger than my 'wisdom' that's watching over my life. In his wisdom I can trust. To this 'the only wise God be glory for ever' (Rom. 16:27).

Great God of mystery, there's no way I can understand you, no way I can tie up all your nature and your purposes in a neat package; you're much too big for that. But one thing I know: you are my God, and in you I trust.

7.

Heaven and the sovereign God

As I start to write this chapter the leaders of the world's most powerful nations are meeting at Gleneagles in Scotland. Their two main items for discussion are the world's poor and the threat to the world's environment through factors causing climate change. Their discussions and decisions have huge potential – for good or for ill – for millions, even billions, of people. Gathered into that one room are men and women who have the power to shape the future of the human race and to determine the fate of our planet.

But now comes news of a series of explosions in London, several on underground trains, and one on a bus. As yet all is confusion, but undoubtedly there have been casualties – terrible injuries and horrific deaths. Who is responsible no-one as yet knows, but it seems clear that the appalling carnage is the work of those who are determined to shape the world the way they want it, and to use any means, including extreme violence, to do so.

Who rules planet earth? Who decides what will happen? Who controls our future? The answer of the human race is, 'We do.' On the personal level I make decisions and choices that shape my future and my life, and, to a considerable extent, the lives of others. On the national and international levels those with power – whether they get it through the ballot box or the gun – have the potential to decide the destiny of nations and of the world itself.

Who rules planet earth? The answer of the Bible is God. The psalmists were in no doubt: 'The LORD reigns, let the nations tremble'; 'God is the King of all the earth... God reigns over the nations... God is seated on his holy throne'; 'The kings of the earth belong to God; he is greatly exalted' (Ps. 99:1, 47:7-8,9).

The throne of God is a key theme of the book of Revelation, where it is mentioned no less than thirty-five times. At a time when the people of God felt they were a small oppressed group at the mercy of the power structures of their day, John is given a vision of heaven. The first thing he sees is the throne of God, with God himself clearly on it (Rev. 4:2-3). The world is not ruled by Rome, or by violence, or by the powers of evil. God is on the throne of the universe.

Revelation chapter 5 introduces us to a scroll in God's right hand; this is the scroll of God's purposes for the world. At first it looks as though the scroll can't be opened, that is, God's purposes cannot be put into effect; the world is out of God's control. John is shattered by this and 'wept and wept.' But then he's told that because Christ has triumphed, he is able to open the scroll (Rev. 5:1-5).

The victory of Christ on the cross has not only made it possible for individuals to find salvation; it has broken the power of all that is evil. In no way will the rebellious powers have the last word. Although God allows them for a time to play out their roles on the stage of history, in the last analysis the affairs of nations and of the world are not in their hands at all, but in the hands of God.

Little wonder that Revelation 5 ends with the praise and worship not just of heaven, but of the whole of creation, singing:

'To him who sits upon the throne and to the Lamb
be praise and honour and glory and power,
    for ever and ever!' (Rev. 5:13)

That was a message that John and the Christians of his day desperately needed to hear. There he was, a prisoner of the Roman authorities, exiled to a lonely island, facing martyrdom. He was desperately concerned for the scattered groups of God's people on the mainland who were facing opposition and persecution, both from the state and from the powers of evil who were determined to destroy them.

Did he have his doubts? Did he struggle with questions about God's wisdom and purposes? Did he wonder how God's people could possibly survive? Some had lost their first love, some were following false teaching, some were facing horrific persecution, some were lukewarm. The powers of evil seemed so strong, the rule of Rome so irresistible. There seemed so little around him to sing about or to give grounds for hope, so little evidence that God was on the throne.

In stark realism the rest of Revelation goes on to depict the dark realities of life on earth: oppression, suffering, death, natural disasters, war, economic injustice, persecution, martyrdom. But again and again the message comes through: though these things are the work of evil rulers or powers of darkness, in no way is God having to stand helplessly by, unable to do anything about them. Instead, in his amazing wisdom and power, these things are actually accomplishing his purposes. It's the cross all over again. Human rulers and demonic powers of darkness conspired together to do the most evil act of all time: to nail the Son of God on to a cross. But God in his sovereign power turned that greatest evil into the world's greatest good, by making the cross the means by which he saved the world and smashed the powers of evil.

Of course we can't always see how God is overruling the decisions and actions of the powers that are at work in our world today. Most of us find it hard to think of what good God may bring out of a terrorist bomb or a natural disaster. But the message of the book of Revelation, and of the whole of the Bible, is that our wise and mighty God is able to bring good out of any event, and that he is committed to doing so. So, as one scene after another unfolds on earth, some of them horrific in the evil and suffering they contain, those who can see behind the events to the control room of heaven can know that whatever may happen, and however evil and inexplicable it may seem in the short term, nothing is beyond the power of God to transform and turn it into something beautiful and good.

The Bible has a truly amazing answer to the problem of the powers that have set themselves up in opposition to God. Instead of giving up and letting them take total control, and instead of blasting them out of existence (a course that would have destroyed me and you), he is allowing them to continue, for a time. He is taking all they do and working it into his own sovereign purposes, so that, when we get to the end of the story, we'll look back and be amazed, both at his incredible wisdom, and at the wonderful things he has brought out of what seemed to be hopelessly evil.

Who rules planet earth? The Bible's answer is God – a sovereign God whose power and wisdom are so great that he can overrule all other powers and bring about his beautiful purposes of grace.

It's very sad that some people find the concept of the sovereignty of God hard to accept. This could be, of course, because they find it threatening: they want to keep for themselves the ultimate control over their lives; in no way do they want to hand it over to God. But there are others who struggle with the philosophical problem. How can God give creatures he has made the freedom to make their own choices and direct their own affairs, and still retain ultimate control of the universe? If that is an issue you are struggling with, here are six things you might try doing.

1. *Check what's driving you.* It's important to check first of all that your problem with the sovereignty of God is an intellectual one, not a personal one. You can do this by answering the question, 'Who do I want to be in control of my life, God or me?'

2. *Accept your limitations.* Accept that though you can't work out the way to reconcile divine sovereignty and human freedom there are others who are more able to do so. Don't make the mistake of saying, 'If I can't understand it, it can't be true.'

3. *Accept the limitations of human understanding.* Realize that even if the wisest philosopher on earth couldn't work out how to solve it, the problem is no problem to an all-wise and all-powerful God.

4. *Keep hold of a big God.* Resist the pressure of our culture to water down your concept of God. Many around us choose to hang on to belief in God, but they make him something less than the God of the Bible – a vague impersonal force, or a creator who has no interest in his creation, or someone who is as helpless in the face

of evil as we are. This is not the God of the Bible. From Genesis to Revelation the description of God is of an all-powerful creator, sovereign over all he has made, and working out his purposes of grace and goodness in all the affairs of the world.

5. *Use the Bible.* Study again the great accounts in the Bible of how God brought good out of what seemed to be disastrous situations: the stories of Joseph and Job, Elijah and Elisha, the exile, the cross, Stephen, the persecution of the early Christians, Paul and all his sufferings. When we're in the thick of it, it's hard to see how God can still be sovereign, but these stories illustrate that no situation is too hard for God.

6. *Look at the big picture.* Every now and then enjoy heaven. Of course we have to share in the struggles and problems here below. But follow John through that door into heaven and spend time seeing things as they truly are. Join the crowd of heavenly worshippers. See the great Creator God on the throne of the universe. Gaze on Jesus, the one who has triumphed over all other powers. Watch him take the scroll of God's purposes and open it stage by stage so that all that happens is woven into his purposes.

> 'Praise and glory
> and wisdom and thanks and honour
> and power and strength
> be to our God for ever and ever.
> Amen!

> 'The kingdom of the world has become the kingdom of our Lord and of his Christ,
>   and he will reign for ever and ever.

'We give thanks to you, Lord God Almighty,
    the One who is and who was,
because you have taken your great power
    and have begun to reign.

'Now have come the salvation and the power and the
kingdom of our God,
    and the authority of his Christ.

'Great and marvellous are your deeds,
    Lord God Almighty.
Just and true are your ways,
    King of the ages.

'Hallelujah!
    For the Lord God Almighty reigns.
Let us rejoice and be glad
    and give him the glory!' (Rev. 7:12, 11:15,17, 12:10,
15:3, 19:6-7)

*That's my God! Big and wise and good; on the
throne of the universe. Take your great power,
Lord, and reign in me and on planet earth. For
yours is the kingdom and the power and the glory,
for ever. Amen.*

8.

The angels and the Creator God

John in his vision saw the sovereign God as he is now, on the throne of the universe. But for this chapter we're going way back in time to the creation of the world, to join the host of heavenly angels as they watched the glory and wonder of the unfolding purposes of the Creator God.

The Bible does not, of course, set out to give an account of the creation of the world in the language of twenty-first century scientists or historians. Had it done so, no-one would have understood it for thousands of years! What it does do is proclaim the fact and the power and the glory of God's creative act in language that is timeless, and as such is absolutely true and dependable.

The best-known description of creation in the Bible comes in the first chapter of Genesis, which gives us a graphic description of an act of creation that is:

- *Deliberate.* For more than a century many scientists have tried to tell us that the whole process of the world coming into being was one of blind meaning-less chance. No-one planned it; nothing directed it. All that is is meaningless and purposeless. We are nothing better than accidents. But recently an increasing number of scientists and thinkers have been rejecting that view, not because they are Christians, but because the scientific evidence simply will not support it. The incredible complexity of the world as it is, and the way it has developed in so short a time (scientifically speaking), make it impossible to see it as a random process. Something – or someone – must have planned it and been in charge. Antony Flew, perhaps the most famous atheist philosopher of the second half of the twentieth century, has recently changed his mind and, persuaded by the scientific evidence, has come to accept the existence of some sort of God. This world is not the product of chance; it is the deliberate creation of an all-powerful God. 'For from him and through him and to him are all things' (Rom. 11:36).

- *Sovereign.* I love the way the Genesis account uses the phrases, 'And God said, "Let there be..." And it was so'(Gen. 1:9). Psalm 33:6 picks up the theme: 'By the word of the LORD were the heavens made, their starry host by the breath of his mouth.' No struggling here with a formidable problem, no labouring over the complexities of creation. Simply a word, a word of power and authority from the almighty sovereign God. This is our God: unwavering, omnipotent, sovereign.

- *Good.* Seven times the creation account pronounces God's creative work 'good'. When he began and made the light, 'God saw that the light was good' (Gen. 1:4). Five times an act of creation is summed up with the phrase, 'And God saw that it was good' (Gen. 1:10,12,18,21,25). In verse 31 at the climax of the chapter, 'God saw all that he had made, and it was very good.' 'Seven' in the Bible speaks of completeness, perfection; just as the seven 'days' cover the whole of God's perfect creative work, so the seven 'good's' emphasize the fullness and perfection of the created order's goodness. 'For everything God created is good' wrote Paul (1 Tim. 4:4); if there is evil in the world it is not God who has put it there.

The Bible constantly returns to the theme of God's great creative acts, often linking his creative power with his continuing sovereignty over the world and the nations and the rebellious powers. For the rest of this chapter we'll use some of the opening words of God's great speech to Job and his friends to focus on one special aspect. There were no human witnesses to God's mighty act of creation, but before he created the material world God had brought into being his heavenly, angelic creation. Just as the angels were witnesses of the amazing mysteries of the coming of God to earth in the incarnation of the Lord Jesus Christ, and of his resurrection from the dead, so they watched with bated breath as God called into being the world that he had planned.

> 'Where were you when I laid the earth's foundation?
>   Tell me, if you understand.
> Who marked off its dimensions? Surely you know!
>   Who stretched a measuring line across it?
> On what were it footings set,
>   or who laid its cornerstone –
> while the morning stars sang together
>   and all the angels shouted for joy?' (Job 38:4-7)

When Christ was born, when God took human form to bring salvation to a lost world, the angels broke out into songs of praise and worship at such an amazing act of grace (Lk. 2:13-14). And when, ages before, God 'laid the earth's foundation' and with words of power brought it into being, the heavens couldn't remain silent; in wonder and praise and worship 'all the angels shouted for joy.'

What was it that got them so excited? And if they were so thrilled at what God had done, why shouldn't we be too? Granted, we've done much to spoil God's creation, but there is still plenty of evidence left of God's glory and the work of his hands for us to get excited about. Here are a few suggestions of ways we can share in the angels' joy.

- *Joy at the power of God's creation.* Psalm 29 describes a thunderstorm, a hurricane that shakes the desert and shatters the mighty trees of the forest. Scientists tell us of the incredible power packed into a space smaller than a pin head that was present at the formation of our universe. This is the power of our God: awesome, glorious, overwhelming. 'In his temple all cry, "Glory!"' (Ps. 29:9). Crashing waves, hurtling planets, exploding supernovas – the God behind these is no small tame dull creator, but someone very big and glorious. Be glad and rejoice; this mighty God, with all the resources of his creative power, is your God and your Father.

- *Joy at the beauty of God's creation.* A blade of grass, a humming bird, one tiny particle of frost. The night sky, the Himalayas, the desert wastes on Mars. The deep places of the earth, dark caves which no-one will ever explore, ocean depths where sunlight never reaches, incredible crystals hidden inside age-old rocks. The new moon, the blazing sun, the deep velvet darkness of night. A child's face, the human body, friendship and love. Our God is beautiful (Ps. 27:4).

He has filled his creation with beauty that reflects his heart and being; gaze upon it, and sing for joy at what he has made and at what he is.

- *Joy at the daring of God's creation.* I don't know what other universes God has created. Maybe he has created just the one, or maybe he has created hundreds. But when the angels saw this universe they saw something that was different from anything that had gone before. God never makes two leaves the same or two atoms identical. This creation was new, bold, and exciting. In his wisdom and his joy God had thought up something new, something breathtaking, exhilarating and thrilling. All the story of planet earth was to climax in a daring new creation, human beings, creatures with the mark of God himself upon them, only a fraction lower than the angels themselves, and 'crowned with glory and honour' (Ps. 8:5). God was to place the responsibility to care for everything else that he had made on to the shoulders of the human race (Gen. 1:28; Ps. 8:6-8), a responsibility it could choose to exercise or reject. Perhaps the angels trembled when they thought of what might happen if the human race failed God's trust; more likely they knew their God well enough to be confident that not even human failure would thwart his daring purposes, and that somehow, if humans failed, God would find a way of redeeming and reclaiming his creation.

- *Joy at the complexity and mystery of God's creation.* The centipede, the incredibly remote galaxies, the intricacy of a grain of dust, DNA, the human mind, time and space. This is no toy, no trivial invention. This is big; it's the work of a big God. See the way a sparrow's feather is formed, and rejoice. Gaze at the Milky Way and shout for joy.

- *Joy at the goodness of God's creation.* The angels rejoiced at the goodness of what they saw. What's more, 'God saw all that he had made, and it was very good' (Gen. 1:31). He saw it and he was glad; his heart went out to it; he rejoiced over it; he loved it. The AV translation of the heavenly song of worship in Revelation 4:11 is, 'Thou art worthy, O Lord, to receive glory and honour and power: for thou hast created all things, and for thy pleasure they are and were created.' It's just as valid a translation as the more recent ones; the song tells us both that creation was by the will of God and that it brought great joy to the heart of God. Don't ignore the brokenness of creation, the damage that human sin has done. But still, with God, find joy in the many expressions of its goodness.

- *Joy at the potential of God's creation.* None of those who watched God's creative work on the day when 'the morning stars sang together and all the angels shouted for joy' knew how the story would continue. Only God knew what was going to happen, that sin would enter this perfect world, that his beautiful creation would be broken and marred, and that it would cost him everything he had to heal it and bring it back to himself. Only God knew that humans, made in his own image, were such that one day he himself would be able to become a man and live in a human body on planet earth. Great was the potential that the angels could see in the world that God had made; greater still was the potential that God could see for redemptive love on a cosmic scale. And still more potential remains. 'The creation waits in eager expectation' for the climax of God's amazing redemptive work, for the day when everything is complete, and 'The kingdom of the world has become the kingdom of our Lord and of his Christ' so that he will reign for ever and ever (Rev. 11:15). Here is something to long for and to look forward to with joy, and to do everything we can to 'speed its coming' (2 Pet. 3:12).

I acknowledge you, Lord, as Creator. This is your world; I am your creature. What you've made is marvellous. I'm thrilled at its beauty and richness and goodness. Praise to the Lord, the Almighty, the King of Creation!

9.

Isaiah and the holy God

One day, perhaps many ages before the creation of the world, God said, 'Let there be living creatures, mighty angels who stand before my throne and see my face. And let them have eyes, eyes to see me and to know and to understand; many eyes, so that they're covered with eyes, in front and behind.' And it was so. And when these living creatures opened their many eyes for the first time, there before them they saw God himself. They gazed on him, and from that moment to this they have never stopped saying:

'Holy, holy, holy
is the Lord God Almighty,
who was and is, and is to come.' (Rev. 4:6-8)

Of course, as they gazed with their many eyes upon God, they could have cried, 'Loving, loving, loving is the Lord God Almighty' or 'Strong, strong, strong is the Lord God Almighty', or 'Wise, wise, wise is the Lord God Almighty.' But what impressed them most and became the theme of their continual hymn of praise was God's holiness.

Back at the time when God called Isaiah to serve him,
Isaiah was given a vision of the heavenly worship.
There, too, the theme was holiness.

> 'Holy, holy, holy is the LORD Almighty;
> the whole earth is full of his glory.' (Is. 6:3)

The impact of the vision of a holy God on Isaiah was
instant and shattering. 'Woe to me!... I am ruined! For I
am a man of unclean lips, and I live among a people of
unclean lips, and my eyes have seen the King, the LORD
Almighty' (Is. 6:5). Then one of the mighty angels took a
burning coal from the fire of the altar of God, and placed
it on the unclean lips of Isaiah, and proclaimed, 'See, this
has touched your lips; your guilt is taken away and your
sin atoned for' (Is. 6:6-7).

The key theme of the worship of God in heaven is his
holiness. The key issue the Bible has to face is how fallen
sinful human creatures can survive in the presence of such
a holy God. For holiness and sin cannot co-exist. Darkness
cannot co-exist with light. A room may be full of darkness,
but once I switch on the light the darkness is destroyed.
But darkness cannot overcome or destroy light (Jn. 1:5 NIV
margin). I may have a container full of darkness; if I open
the container in a lighted room, in no way will the darkness rush out of the container and make the room dark.
Instead, the light instantly destroys the darkness.

It is the same with God's holiness; there's no way our
sin can overcome it; the only possibility is that it should
overcome and destroy our sin. As Isaiah knew, if God's
holiness is to destroy my sin, it will have to destroy me
too because I'm sinful – unless God somehow finds a
way of dealing with my sin.

Throughout the Bible the holiness of God is stressed
again and again. He is the Holy One of Israel (Ps. 71:22);

his Spirit is the Holy Spirit (Ps. 51:11); Jesus is the Holy One of God (Mk. 1:24). His call to his people was that they must be holy, because he is holy (Lev. 11:44). The Old Testament sacrificial system was put in place to remove the defilement of the people before God. We too, in New Testament times, are called to be a 'holy priesthood', a 'holy nation' (1 Pet. 2:5,9). 'Without holiness', says the writer to the Hebrews, 'no-one will see the Lord' (Heb. 12:14). God chose us in Christ before the creation of the world, that we should be holy (Eph. 1:4).

Those who have studied the meaning of the Old Testament word for holiness tell us that its root meaning is separation from sin. Whilst this may be helpful there is a risk that it can lead us to a basically negative idea of holiness. A holy person, we might conclude, is someone who keeps away from sin, who doesn't tell lies or commit adultery or hate or steal. Similarly, God is holy because he doesn't do any of these things either.

Though, of course, there's some truth here, such a view of holiness is hopelessly inadequate. It's like trying to describe a lion simply by saying it lacks the characteristics of a mouse. Holiness is much more than the lack of sin. In no way is it a negative thing; it is gloriously, magnificently positive. What Isaiah glimpsed was powerful, dynamic, burning. It was like the heat of the sun, radiating out with irresistible power and energy; nothing in its path could withstand it or escape it.

As the heat of the sun either burns and destroys or warms and gives life, so God's holiness either destroys what is unholy, or shares its purity and goodness with whatever will welcome and receive it. Isaiah was right to tremble as he stood in his sinfulness before the holy God; in a sense he was right to speak of ruin, since he was indeed a sinful man, and he was to be called to declare a message of destruction and ruin to the sinful people of

God. But he was wrong to despair. God's holiness does not have to destroy; where we are willing to receive it it will cleanse and transform and make us holy. Even the ruined cities, the land judged for its sinfulness, the broken people of God, can one day be made clean and holy through the mighty power of the holy and sovereign God (Is. 61:1-11).

Isaiah's vision of the holiness of God and his cleansing and equipping for service formed the basis of his ministry. How much has the holiness of God meant for you? How much impact has it had on your life? How much is it affecting you now? Here are some suggestions that may help you.

1. *Realize the significance of the holiness of God.* God has many attributes, and we may be tempted to feel we can't major on them all. So we make a lot of his love, or his grace, and leave his holiness to others. But this won't do. Holiness isn't a minor attribute of God that we can safely ignore. It's foundational to all that he is. If we ignore it or play it down we will have a disastrously inaccurate picture of God. Without it we will hardly be able to make sense of the Bible's teaching on salvation or on God's purposes for the world. So spend time getting to grips with what holiness really means. Ask the Holy Spirit to teach you; read the Bible accounts of those who met this holy God; watch Jesus as he lived true holiness in a human body amidst all the pressures of daily life.

2. *Encounter the holiness of God.* Go a stage further. Experience the real thing. For most of us this is an urgent need. We find it easy to take God's holiness lightly because we so rarely meet the holy God. Rarely do we stand on 'holy ground'. Rarely do we

fall before God and cry, 'Go away from me, Lord; I am a sinful man!' (Lk. 5:8). Rarely do we fall at his feet as though dead (Rev. 1:17). How do we encounter his holiness? Not by our own engineering; such revelation has to come from God himself. But put yourself in the way of it. Cry out to God for it. Be ready for it when it comes.

3. *Tremble before the holiness of God*. Of course we come with confidence to God's throne of grace, into the presence of the Lord 'the Most Holy Place by the blood of Jesus' (Heb. 4:16, 10:19). But hand in hand with that confidence should be an awareness that the One who welcomes us is the holy God, whose eyes burn with fire, and who knows the secrets of our hearts. The Holy Place is holy, and those who enter need to bow before the One who is there.

4. *Receive the holiness of God*. There's something in all of us that persistently gets the issue of holiness and God the wrong way round. The universal tendency is to assume that holiness has to come first and then God comes second. That is, we have to sort out our sinful lives and get to a point where we are holy, or at least less unholy, and then God will be pleased with us and come to us. The experience of Isaiah was the exact opposite. In no way did he sort out the unholiness of his life before God came to him. The holy God came to him, and in his holiness did what was necessary to make him holy. It's back to the heat of the sun. I don't have to warm myself up to enjoy summer sunshine. All I have to do is get out into the sunshine and let it warm me up. I like the picture in Psalm 48:10 of God's right hand 'filled with righteousness.' God reaches out to us, and to the ends of the earth, with his mighty

right hand overflowing with saving, cleansing righteousness. It is there for the taking. Don't wait until
you feel you are good enough to receive it; receive
him, and with him receive his gift of forgiveness,
righteousness and holiness.

5. *Live the holiness of God.* God's holiness is not just for
receiving; it is for living. God makes us holy so that we
may express that holiness in who we are and the way
we live. The 'sanctifying work of the Spirit', that is, the
work of the Spirit that makes us holy, has to be followed
by 'obedience to Jesus Christ' and holiness in all we do
(1 Pet. 1:2,14-15). God has made us clean and pure; we
stand before him as holy children of a holy God. So
now we must be clean and pure in all that we do; we
must show the world that we are holy children of a
holy God. Maybe we'll find it tough; it always seems to
be easier to slip back into sin than to keep ourselves
pure. But we have the promise of the Holy Spirit to
empower and equip us, and when we do fail we can
turn back to God for his cleansing and renewing grace.

6. *Spread the holiness of God.* Our culture is full of unholiness. Sin and corruption and perversion are all
around us. But if it's true that light is stronger than
darkness, part of our task in the world is to spread the
light of God's holiness. As Jesus put it in the Sermon
on the Mount, we're 'the light of the world'; light isn't
for hiding but for shining so that everyone can benefit from it. The light of our lives is to shine out to those
around us, so that 'they may see your good deeds and
praise your Father in heaven' (Mt. 5:14-16). Leave
others to spread despair or to be moulded by the culture around us; live your life so that those around you
may encounter the holiness of God.

Lord, please show me your holiness. Make me know what it means to have a holy God. Come, fill me with your holy presence and make me holy. Destroy my sin; teach me to live a holy life; by your Holy Spirit empower me that I may be holy because you are holy.

10.

Sinai and the awesome God

God is one. That means his character is one. The different facets of his nature make up one perfect whole; in no way do any of them stand alone. So, for example, God is love and he is also holy. His love and his holiness aren't kept separate, operating in different spheres. Every time God loves, it is with a holy love. Every expression of God's holiness is of loving holiness. Though for the convenience of our understanding we separate out the different elements of his nature, in reality they can't ever be separated.

God is awesome. Again and again, from Genesis to Revelation, when people met him they were overwhelmed by who he was. When God met Jacob in a dream, he was afraid and declared, 'How awesome is this place!' (Gen. 28:17). Ezekiel fell face down before 'the appearance of the likeness of the glory of the LORD' (Ezek. 1:28). The shepherds in the fields in the Christmas story were terrified when the angel of the Lord came to them (Lk. 2:9). Saul of Tarsus and John fell to the ground when confronted with the exalted Christ (Acts 9:4; Rev. 1:17).

Of course God is awesome. If a hurricane or a thunderstorm is awesome, if the deep places of the ocean or the vastness of space are awesome, how much more awesome is the One who made them. Everything about him is awesome. His power is awesome; his glory and holiness are awesome. The length and the breadth and the height and the depth of his love are awesome. His truth and his purposes are awesome. There is nothing about him that is small, petty, trivial. Everything about him is awesome.

According to the Bible, the right reaction to the awesomeness of God is fear. But some people have problems with the concept of fear when it is applied to our relationship with God. They have no problem loving God, or obeying God, or trusting God; but they feel that our relationship with God as Christians is such that fear should have no place in it. 'Why should we fear our loving Heavenly Father?' they say; 'God has not given us a spirit of fear' (2 Tim. 1:7); 'there's no fear in love: "perfect love drives out fear"' (1 Jn. 4:18). Of course they're right to reject anything that would deny the confidence and trust that we have as we approach our Heavenly Father. But we should not ignore the fact that the Bible does talk about fearing God, not only in the Old Testament, but in the New Testament as well.

Paul encourages us to put into practice the salvation God has given us 'with fear and trembling' (Phil. 2:12). He also speaks of the fear of God when encouraging the Corinthian Christians to live holy lives, though the NIV translates his words, 'perfecting holiness out of reverence for God' (2 Cor. 7:1). He speaks too of our 'fear of Christ', though, again, the NIV translates his words as 'reverence for Christ' (Eph. 5:21). Elsewhere the New Testament commands us to 'fear God' (1 Pet. 2:17), and to 'worship God acceptably with reverence and awe' (Heb. 12:28).

Clearly then, fear – the right kind of fear – is something we should feel in our relationship with our awesome God. But how do we know what is the right kind? The NIV gives us some clues by the way it translates the common New Testament word 'fear', using terms like 'reverence', 'respect', 'worship', 'awe' and 'reverent fear'. A Christian shouldn't feel terror or alarm before God; this would ignore many of the other great aspects of God that have been revealed to us, especially in the Lord Jesus. The right kind of fear is a fear that sits comfortably with all the other things we know about him. It is a reverent awareness of who he truly is; a right response of a human creature, loved and redeemed at infinite cost, to the great and glorious God.

So God's awesomeness in no way contradicts his grace and goodness and love; indeed, his grace and goodness and love are themselves awesome. If we tremble before him it is because we realize how vast is his grace, how utter his goodness, how astounding his love; we rightly fear lest we belittle them or scorn them or grieve the heart of the One who is so wonderful towards us.

Though there was yet much more that God had to reveal to his people about his nature and ways, right at the start of his dealings with those he had rescued from Egypt, God gave them a dramatic experience of his awesomeness at Mount Sinai (Ex. 19:1-20:21). For the rest of this chapter we'll stand with them before the mountain, and learn what we can about this awesome God of ours, supplementing it where we need to with the fuller revelation of his nature that we have in Jesus.

- *The awesomeness of God is inseparable from his grace.* Before God descended upon Mount Sinai, he reminded his people of how it was they came to that point, how he rescued them from Egypt, how he carried them on eagles' wings, and brought them to himself to be a 'treasured possession', a 'kingdom of priests and a holy nation' (Ex. 19:3-6). All his dealings with them had been in love and grace; it was in the same love and grace that he was now going to show them his glory and awesomeness.

- *The awesomeness of God arises from his nearness.* A thunderstorm a thousand miles away doesn't affect us; one right over our heads certainly does. 'I am going to come to you,' said God to Moses; 'the LORD will come down on Mount Sinai in the sight of all the people' (Ex. 19:9,11). If we have a distant remote God it's unlikely we'll find him awesome. Those whose God is just an impersonal force will hardly tremble before it. But our God is a God who comes, who draws near in his glory and greatness. It's then we realize how big he is, and bow before him in awe and worship.

- *The awesomeness of God calls us to holiness.* If we're casual about God we'll be casual about holiness too. But God is a holy God, and he's not casual about holiness (Ex. 19:10). In wisdom and grace God showed his people his awesomeness, so that they would take him and all he said seriously. I guess we need that, too, lest we take God and God's commands too lightly.

- *The awesomeness of God reminds us of limits.* When he gave the law God put limits around Mount Sinai (Ex. 19:12); the law itself put strict limits on what God's people could and could not do. The New Testament makes it plain that many of the limits that applied in Old Testament times have now been removed. The curtain in the temple, dividing us from God, has been torn down; we can enter boldly into the 'Most Holy Place' (Mk. 15:38; Heb. 10:19). There are no limits to his grace or love or mercy; no barriers between us and him. But that is not to say that anything goes, that there are no limits. 'Shall we go on sinning, so that grace may increase?' asked Paul (Rom. 6:1). Of course not, he replied. True, if we did there would be no limit to God's grace and forgiveness; but there's no way we who are his children would want to trade on his graciousness by grieving his heart. If we're tempted to feel that because of our freedom in Christ anything goes, we need to remember who it is we're dealing with. This is no doddery deity we can hoodwink or play around with; this is the living God, into whose hands it is a dreadful thing to fall, whom we're called to worship 'with reverence and awe, for our "God is a consuming fire"' (Heb. 12:28-29).

- *In the awesomeness of God we meet him.* Moses led the people to the foot of the mountain 'to meet with God' (Ex. 19:17). With Isaiah we meet God in his holiness; with Job we meet the fantastic God; in Jesus we meet the Father. This is not three Gods, but one. At Sinai we meet God in his awesomeness, but it's still the same God. Don't run from his awesomeness; don't seek to avoid it; let him come to you with smoke and fire, with thunder and the sound of a trumpet – and there meet your God.

- *At the awesomeness of God nature trembles.* So far we've been focusing on how we as Christians react to the awesomeness of God. But the Bible has plenty to say about the relation of the rest of God's creation to his awesomeness. Mount Sinai trembled violently and was covered with smoke (Ex. 19:18). If these disciples don't worship me, said Jesus to the crowds on Palm Sunday, the very 'stones will cry out' (Lk. 19:40). A few days later, as he hung on the cross, nature itself trembled, and the land was plunged into darkness (Mt. 27:45). When he returns the whole created order will be disrupted (Mk. 13:24-25). The world around us is not some self-created and self-perpetuating machine; it is God's creation, and God holds it in being. Though it can't know God as we do, in its own way it worships and trembles before his greatness and awesomeness.

- *Our awesome God tells us, 'Do not be afraid.'* Hardly words we would expect as we read through the story. Everything so far seems to be designed to make the people afraid; indeed, verses 18-19 make it clear that all the people were very afraid: when they saw what was going on they kept well away and 'trembled with fear.' But God tells them to stop. Rightly they are filled with awe at the coming of so great and so holy a God; but God has come so that he can be with them and they can know his presence and goodness and grace. As in so many of the accounts where God comes to his people, God comforts and strengthens them and tells them to set their fear of his presence aside. Here, again, is the balance the Bible teaches: it is right to tremble and fear at the awesomeness of God but it is wrong to let that fear dominate our relationship with him.

- *The awesomeness of God must keep us from sinning.* 'Don't be afraid' he said; 'but don't forget the fear of God; let it continue to be "with you to keep you from sinning"' (Ex. 20:20). Sadly, the people ignored his words; their memories were short, and by the time Moses came down from the mountain, the people had forgotten their fear of God and were worshipping a golden calf (Ex. 32).

If you're like me, you'll need all the help you can get to keep you from sinning. There's plenty of help available from the Holy Spirit, from the Bible, and from other people. But here's an additional source of help: remembering the awesomeness of the God before whose presence we live.

Great and mighty God, awesome in majesty, glorious beyond my wildest imagining, I fall at your feet in worship and wonder. You are so great, so overwhelming, so fearsome. Wonder of wonders, you are my God. Teach me to tremble before you in holy awe, and to live before you as one who truly belongs to so awesome a God.

11.

Jesus and the Father God

If you want to see what God is like, look at Jesus. 'Anyone who has seen me has seen the Father,' he said in answer to Philip's request in the upper room to show his disciples the Father (Jn. 14:9). It's in Jesus that we have the fullest and clearest revelation of who God is and what he's like. In this chapter we're going to look at one aspect, the way Jesus revealed God as our Father.

One of the most remarkable things about Jesus was the way he prayed. His disciples were all used to praying, and were familiar with the prayers of the Old Testament and the synagogue worship. But Jesus prayed differently; his relationship with God was different from anything the disciples had seen before. The difference was summed up in the way he began his prayers, the way he addressed God. In contrast to the Old Testament and universal Jewish practice, he spoke to God as 'Abba'.

'Abba' was a familiar Aramaic word in the time of Jesus. Its origin was in baby-talk; just as the earliest words spoken by babies in the English speaking world are 'da-da' and 'ma-ma', so the first words of Jewish babies were 'Abba' (daddy) and 'Imma' (mummy). But, unlike 'da-da', 'Abba' was used beyond babyhood. It was a familiar word on the lips of adults as they spoke to their fathers with warmth and affection, expressing love and trust and a close deep relationship.

This was the word Jesus used when speaking to God. Those who heard it were amazed. Occasionally in the Old Testament God was called 'Father' in the context of his relationship to the nation of Israel, though never in his relationship to ordinary individuals. Some of the Jewish prayers of the first century AD also spoke of 'Our Father, the King', but neither the Old Testament nor the Jewish prayers used the concept of God's fatherhood in such a daring way as Jesus did. For them the concept described God's general fatherhood of the Jewish nation; he was the one who had brought them into being as a nation and watched over them with fatherly concern and authority. But Jesus' use of 'Abba' spoke of a deep warm personal relationship of love and trust, something radical and new.

The obvious explanation for this, of course, is that God is Jesus' Father in a unique way. When Jesus prayed 'Abba', he was the divine Son addressing his Father, the second person of the Trinity expressing the profound and beautiful relationship he had had with God since before the foundation of the world. As that is so, we might conclude, the word Jesus used and the way he spoke must be limited to him alone, since he alone is in that deepest of all relationships.

But, amazingly, not only did Jesus use 'Abba' in speaking to his Father, he taught his disciples to use it too when they came to him and asked him to teach them how they should pray. And he didn't wait until they were mature super-saints; he told them to do it when they were right at the beginning of their relationship with God: theologically ignorant, far from holy, and still weak in their faith and commitment.

Among all the wonderful things Jesus showed us about God, this surely is the most wonderful: we can have a deep warm personal relationship of love and trust with him, not because we've earned the right to it, but because he desires it and makes it possible. To each of us the eternal God, sovereign and holy, glorious and mighty, says, 'Call me Abba. Speak to me as Jesus spoke; experience my nearness and goodness and love as he did.' God has made us his children, his sons and daughters. He has put his Spirit in our hearts; just like Jesus we can call him 'Abba' (Rom. 8:15-17; Gal. 4:6-7).

This amazing new revelation must not, of course, push out of focus all the other aspects of God's nature that are revealed in the Bible. This new insight about God is given to enrich everything else the Bible has taught about him, not to replace it. So, instead of concluding that God isn't any longer awesome because he's our Father, we need to take on board the much larger truth that the awesome, glorious Creator God – holy, mysterious, fantastic, great beyond our wildest imaginings – is also our Father. The One whom we can address as 'Abba', with whom we can have a deep and loving personal relationship is the mighty sovereign Lord over all.

'Lord, show us the Father,' asked Philip in John 14:9, just after Jesus had stated that he is the 'the way and the truth and the life.' As he sat talking with his disciples in that upper room Jesus kept returning to the theme of the Father and his relationship with him and his followers' relationship with him:

> 'Don't you believe that I am in the Father, and that the Father is in me?... Believe me when I say that I am in the Father and the Father is in me... Before long... you will realise that I am in my Father, and you are in me, and I am

in you. Whoever has my commands and obeys them, he is the one who loves me. He who loves me will be loved by my Father, and I too will love him and show myself to him.... If anyone loves me, he will obey my teaching. My Father will love him, and we will come to him and make our home with him.' (Jn. 14:10,11,19,20-21,23)

How much do you know of what Jesus is speaking about here? How deep is your relationship with God? Do you truly know him as Abba Father? Are the Father and Son so near and real to you that you can describe them as having made their home in your life? If you're not sure of these things, why not work through the following five points, each based on the teaching of Jesus in the upper room, recorded in John 14.

1. *Start with Jesus*. He is the way, the only way to the Father (verse 6). When we find him, we find the Father; when we know Jesus, we know God (verse 9). Not only does he show God to us; through his death and resurrection he has broken down the barrier between us and God and becomes the way into his presence. So draw near to Jesus; read about him; think about him; get to know him; sit with him on the hillside or in the upper room; listen to his voice, know his nearness.

2. *Live Jesus*. Four times in ten verses Jesus links together two closely related themes, that of loving him and obeying his commands or his teaching (verses 15, 21, 23 and 24). Here he's moving beyond simply knowing a lot about him, or even knowing him personally. If we have a relationship with him it will affect us deeply, and change our lives. We shall love him, and that love will be expressed in the way we live. When

Jesus talks about obeying his commands, he's not taking us back to the Old Testament law, where people believed that their relationship with God depended on their strict obedience to every command of God. The word he uses means 'watch' rather than 'keep in every detail.' After all, he knew as well as we do that none of us could fulfil the new command he had just given, to 'love one another' as he has loved us (Jn. 13:34). But what he was calling his disciples to do was to make that command the basis of their living, to build all that they were and all that they did on his teaching. Check your life. Is Jesus so important to you that you make his teaching and commands the basis for all you are and do?

3. *Welcome the Holy Spirit.* We have that deep relationship with the Father that is expressed in the cry of '*Abba*, Father', says Paul, because we have 'received the Spirit' (Rom. 8:15), the 'Spirit of his Son' which God has sent into our hearts (Gal. 4:6). In the upper room, Jesus promised the coming of the Holy Spirit to live and be in his disciples (Jn. 14:16-17). The three persons of the Godhead cannot be separated; if we have a deep relationship with Jesus, then we will have a deep relationship with the Father; if the Son and the Father are to be in us, then the Spirit will be in us too. So open your life again to the Holy Spirit of God; welcome him in; open up each part to him – your mind, your beliefs, your attitudes, your relationships, your problems, your ambitions, your body, your actions, your words. 'Be filled with the Spirit' (Eph. 5:18).

4. *Accept the promise of Jesus.* 'If anyone loves me, he will obey my teaching. My Father will love him, and we

will come to him and make our home with him'
(Jn. 14:23). These are amazing words. Here is the holy
God, the sovereign Creator, the Lord of the universe,
the wonderful, mysterious, awesome King over all,
and in the clearest and simplest words he says he will
come to us and make his home with us. What's more,
he'll do it in love. Of course there may be places
where his holy presence will have to judge and deal
with aspects of our lives; of course he'll come in
power and glory and truth. But all his coming is in
love. And maybe there's another point here. Not only
does he come in love, he loves to be in us, to be at
home in our lives, to be our Abba Father, to have us
as his child, to enjoy that deep and close relationship.

5. *Live as the child of your Father.* God is with you. The
   Mighty God is in you. Your Heavenly Father is closer
   to you than anything else. The King of the universe
   has made his home in your heart, body and life. Stop
   living then as though you are on your own. Stop living as though your mind or your body is yours to do
   what you like with. Stop dabbling in sin. Stop worry-
   ing. Start letting your Father take over each part of
   your life. Start trusting him to keep and guide and
   give you all you need (Mt. 6:32). Start enjoying his
   presence throughout the day. Talk to him; cry out to
   him when things are tough; thank him and praise him
   when your life is rich with his blessings. Listen for his
   voice through the Spirit; be filled with his peace
   through Jesus (Jn. 14:26-27).

*Come, Holy Spirit, Spirit of Christ, show me what
it means to cry, 'Abba, Father.' Give me that
confidence that I am a child of God; give me that
trust that knows I am in my Father's hands.*

Come, Father, and make your home in me. Through Jesus my Lord speak your truth into my life that I may walk in your ways and grow deeper and deeper in your love.

12.

Hagar and the God who cares

She was only a slave, picked up cheap, maybe when Abraham and Sarah were in Egypt. But she had her uses, to run here and there at the beck and call of her mistress, and to provide a sexual outlet for her master. Then she got pregnant, and relationships between her and the barren Sarah became strained. But she was dispensable, even though she was carrying Abraham's child. 'Do with her whatever you think best,' said Abraham. 'Then Sarai ill-treated Hagar; so she fled from her' (Gen. 16:6).

And that would have been that. Except that God was watching. And caring. Through an angel he showed himself to Hagar, and told her to go back to her mistress. There were still tough times ahead, but God was watching over her, and had purposes of grace and goodness for her. So Hagar gave God a name, 'the God who sees me'; the place where she met him she called 'the well of the Living One who sees me' (Gen. 16:7-14). Years later there was a re-run of the whole story. Hagar and her son, rejected again by Abraham, were dying of thirst in the desert. Again God intervened; again their lives were spared (Gen. 21:8-21).

It's a strange old story, but it picks up a theme which comes again and again in the Bible. The compiler of Genesis is telling us the story of Abraham; his concern is the purposes of God through him and his line through his legitimate son, Isaac. For him Hagar, the Egyptian slave, is only an incidental, effectively a dead-end. But not for God. This God, the God of Abraham and of Isaac, wasn't just watching over his chosen servants. He was 'the God who sees,' and he saw Hagar and her child every bit as much as he saw Abraham and Isaac.

The word Hagar used when she named God 'the God who sees me' is a common Old Testament word for seeing. But, like many Hebrew words, there's more to it than a straight translation would suggest. There was something very practical about the Hebrew mind, something that reflected the practicality of the mind of their God. It wasn't a case of God seeing Hagar and her need and 'passing by on the other side.' For God to see is to care, to do something, to act, to provide. 'I have indeed seen the misery of my people in Egypt,' said God to Moses. 'So I have come down to rescue them' (Ex. 3:7,8). So 'the God who sees' is the God who cares, and who acts in compassion and grace.

God watched over and cared for the slave, the outcast, the reject. That's our God. All through the Old Testament this is a recurring theme, as God commands his people to care for 'the alien, the fatherless, and the widow.' 'Never forget,' he said, 'that you were once slaves yourselves in Egypt. So care for those who are slaves and at the bottom of the pile. Be concerned for them. Make special provision for them. Never take advantage of them.'

'Do not take advantage of a hired man who is poor and needy, whether he is a brother Israelite or an alien living in one of your towns... Do not deprive the alien or the fatherless of justice, or take the cloak of the widow as a pledge. Remember that you were slaves in Egypt and the LORD your God redeemed you from there. That is why I command you to do this.

'When you are harvesting in your field and you overlook a sheaf, do not go back to get it. Leave it for the alien, the fatherless and the widow, so that the LORD your God may bless you in all the work of your hands. When you beat the olives from your trees, do not go over the branches a second time. Leave what remains for the alien, the fatherless and the widow. When you harvest the grapes in your vineyard, do not go over the vines again. Leave what remains for the alien, the fatherless and the widow. Remember that you were slaves in Egypt. That is why I command you to do this.' (Deut. 24:14, 17-22)

In the New Testament the picture is the same. Of course God cares for the important people, the rulers, the priests, the Pharisees. But at the start of the gospel story it's despised shepherds who are told of the birth of the Saviour, and at the end it's a broken woman who is met by the risen Christ in the garden. All through his ministry Jesus showed a special concern for the outcasts and rejects of society: tax collectors and 'sinners' and those who were 'sick' were his speciality (Lk. 5:30-31).

God sees and cares. He sees the starving children in Africa. He sees the poor in South America. He sees the oppressed, the slaves and the refugees. He sees those who are 'without hope and without God in the world' (Eph. 2:12). He sees those who have never heard the good news of Jesus. And he cares. His heart goes out to them. And he calls his people to see as he sees and to care as he cares.

There's an interesting twist to the story of Hagar in Genesis 16. God sees and cares; he meets with Hagar and speaks to her. For the rest of her life she was able to say,

'I have now seen the One who sees me' (Gen. 16:13). But meeting with God and knowing the care of God didn't solve all her problems.

I guess we all have a tendency to feel that if God sees the mess I'm in and cares about me, and does something, then the thing he does must solve my problem. If I'm a slave, he must set me free. If I'm ill, he must make me better. If I've got a bad boss, he must move him or her to another department.

But that's not the way it was with Hagar. Hagar was running away from the cruelty she had experienced at the hands of Sarah; surely, we might think, if God cares for her he'll make her a free woman, maybe even with some slaves of her own thrown in for good measure. But instead God said, 'Go back to your mistress and submit to her' (Gen. 16:9).

Though God also gave her a promise of the birth of her son, and of descendants 'too numerous to count', the future he offered her was far from easy. Her son, Ishmael, 'will be a wild donkey of a man; his hand will be against everyone and everyone's hand against him' (Gen. 16:12). Where, we might feel, is the evidence of the caring heart of God in all that?

The answer is that when God sees and cares, he sees far more than you or I could possibly see, and his care is expressed in ways far more profound than we can ever understand. When as a child I broke a neighbour's window or skipped my homework, my ardent prayer was 'God, don't let anyone find out' or 'God, make the teacher ill.' In my narrow way of seeing things, if God really cared for me, he'd get me out the mess.

But God saw further. He knew the neighbour couldn't afford to get the window repaired; he wanted the teacher in the peak of condition; he knew what damage it would do to me if I found that I could be lazy and get away with it every time. And because he cared for the neighbour and the teacher and for me, he didn't get me out of the mess. It was 'go back and face the music.'

'Cast all your anxiety on him,' wrote Peter, 'because he cares for you.' But in the next breath he was writing about the ongoing suffering his readers had to face. In the long run, the future was bright, but in no way did God's care guarantee an easy ride. So, he says, we need to humble ourselves 'under God's mighty hand, that he may lift you up in due time' (1 Pet. 5:6-11).

Here are a few things we can learn from Hagar, and from the God who saw her and cared for her and met her in the desert.

- *God sees.* God knows and cares about each of us and all the details of our lives. Many times we're not aware that he's watching over us; sometimes we struggle with doubts and begin to think he must have forgotten us. But the God who watched over the outcast slave in the desert never ceases to watch over you.

  > Why do you say, O Jacob,
  >   and complain, O Israel,
  > 'My way is hidden from the LORD;
  >   my cause is disregarded by my God?'
  > Do you not know?
  >   Have you not heard?
  > The Lord is the everlasting God,
  >   the Creator of the ends of the earth.
  > He will not grow tired or weary,
  >   and his understanding no-one can fathom.
  >   (Is. 40:27-28)

- *God cares for those who are suffering.* He cares for everyone, but he has a particular care for the hurting, the oppressed, the poor, the rejects, those who are at the bottom of the pile. The world contains millions of such people. I guess there are a few in your street, too: people with disabilities, those who are psychologically damaged, children of broken homes, the lonely, those trapped in poverty, prostitutes and those who are slaves of their sexuality, and many more. These are the contemporary equivalents of the Old Testament 'aliens'.

- *God's care means we care.* Because God cares for those at the bottom of the pile, he expects us to care for them too.

- *The outcome of God's care for us won't always be what we expect or want.* He sees far more than we see; 'his understanding no-one can fathom.' He's committed to our long-term good, but that may mean that the result of his care in the short term may be something we wouldn't choose and can't understand. In those cases we will gain nothing by struggling against him, or complaining. In humility we need to give way and trust his wisdom and goodness.

We've said that our God is always practical. He doesn't see what needs to be done, and then do nothing. As you come to the end of this chapter with its reminder of how much God cares about those who are hurting, perhaps you need to take some action now that will express that care. It could be help at the local centre for the homeless, or an offer to babysit for a single mum. It doesn't have to be anything dramatic; you'll probably make more progress if you choose to befriend one child who is at risk than if you decide to solve the teenage drug problem of your city. But doing just one thing is far better than seeing the need and doing nothing.

*It's so good, Lord, to know that you see and care
and act on what you see. I bless you that you
know me inside out; nothing is beyond your
wisdom and love and power; I don't need to worry
about anything. Please go on watching over my
life and showing me your ways step by step, even
when the path is tough. And as you care so
tremendously for me, please let your care flow
through me to others, for the glory of your name
and the coming of your kingdom.*

13.

John and the love of God

John in his gospel doesn't mention himself by name. But every now and then he mentions an unnamed disciple of Jesus, who is almost certainly John himself. He first appears in John 1:35-40 as one of the two first followers of Jesus. He had been a disciple of John the Baptist, and one day John the Baptist pointed out Jesus as he was passing. 'Look,' he said, 'the Lamb of God!' John and Andrew instantly followed Jesus, who turned and asked them what they wanted. Their answer, 'Where are you staying?' effectively meant that what they wanted was time with Jesus, to go with him to where he was living, where they could learn from him without interruption. Jesus replied by inviting them to spend the day with him. That was the moment that changed John's life, his first meeting with Jesus, and he carefully records the time at which it happened: 'It was about the tenth hour.'

Later in his gospel John refers several times to himself as 'the disciple whom Jesus loved' (Jn. 13:23, 19:26, 20:2, 21:7,20). In no way is this meant to suggest that Jesus didn't love his other disciples, or that Jesus loved John more than he loved the others (see Jn. 13:1, 15:9). It was probably a nickname given by the other disciples to express the closeness of the relationship between Jesus and John. We all know people who find it hard to receive love or to express love; John was the opposite of that; even before he had grasped the full implications of who Jesus was he had with him a deep relationship of holy love.

Not surprisingly, then, the theme of love comes up again and again in the three letters that have traditionally been attributed to John. Indeed there are as many references to love in these three short letters as there are in all the letters of Paul put together. Much of the time John is writing about the love that we must show for one another, but he makes it abundantly clear that our love, whether it's love for God or for others, is based on God's love for us. 'We love,' he says, 'because he first loved us' (1 Jn. 4:19).

> How great is the love the Father has lavished on us, that we should be called children of God!... God is love. This is how God showed his love among us: he sent his one and only Son into the world that we might live through him. This is love: not that we loved God, but that he loved us and sent his Son as an atoning sacrifice for our sins. (1 Jn. 3:1, 4:8-10)

The theme of the love of God runs all through the Bible. In the Old Testament it is mostly expressed in terms of his love for his chosen people. God 'loved your forefathers,' said Moses to the Israelites, 'and chose their descendants after them... The LORD did not set his affection on you and choose you because you were more numerous than other peoples, for you were the fewest of all peoples. But it was because the LORD loved you' (Deut. 4:37, 7:7-8). God calls his love for his people 'an everlasting love' (Jer. 31:3); it didn't depend on circumstances or even on the people's response. The book of

Hosea graphically pictures the consistency of God's love despite the unfaithfulness of the people. As Hosea continued to show his love for his unfaithful wife, so God's love for his people cannot be destroyed even by their flagrant sin, which cried out for justice and punishment.

'When Israel was a child, I loved him,
    and out of Egypt I called my son.
But the more I called Israel,
    the further they went from me.
They sacrificed to the Baals
    and they burned incense to images.
It was I who taught Ephraim to walk,
    taking them by the arms;
but they did not realise
    it was I who healed them.
I led them with cords of human kindness,
    with ties of love;
I lifted the yoke from their neck
    and bent down to feed them.

'How can I give you up, Ephraim?
    How can I hand you over, Israel?

'My heart is changed within me;
    all my compassion is aroused.
I will not carry out my fierce anger,
    nor will I turn and devastate Ephraim.
For I am God and not man –
    the Holy One among you.
    I will not come in wrath.' (Hos. 11:1-4, 8-9)

Though the focus in the Old Testament is on God's love for his chosen people, there are hints that his love is in fact much broader, for example in Psalm 145:

The LORD is gracious and compassionate,
　slow to anger and rich in love.
The LORD is good to all;
　he has compassion on all he has made. (Ps. 145:8-9)

The universality of God's love is clearly taught in the New Testament, both by the life of Jesus, who demonstrated love to Gentiles as well as to Jews, and by specific teaching. 'God demonstrates his own love for us in this' wrote Paul to the Gentile Romans, 'while we were yet sinners, Christ died for us' (Rom. 5:8). 'All of us,' he wrote to the Ephesians, meaning Jews and Gentiles alike, '...were by nature objects of wrath. But because of his great love for us, God, who is rich in mercy, made us alive with Christ' (Eph. 2:3-5). And John himself famously stated, 'God so loved the world that he gave his one and only Son' (Jn. 3:16). The measure of God's love for the whole world is the incarnation and cross of the second person of the Trinity; nothing could be greater than that.

As we've seen in chapter 10, there's no way we should take any one of the facets of God's nature and isolate it from the others. However profound and glorious the love of God is we need to remember that it is a holy love, an awesome love, a sovereign love, a mysterious love, and so on. This will save us from the mistake of patterning our image of God's love on our own concepts and experiences of love, or of picturing his love as something sloppy and undiscerning.

It's significant that in the passage from Hosea God specifically says that it is his holiness that lies behind his love, and in these days when we rightly stress that God's love does not depend on our goodness, we need to remember that his love is always holy love. The father in the story of the lost son loved his boy despite all he had done, but in no way did he love or condone his sin.

'God is love,' wrote the beloved disciple. Why not come with John as he re-lives his memories of Jesus, and drink again with him at the river of his love?

- *On a hot day in Samaria.* She was a reject, a Samaritan, a woman, sexually defiled. As far as John and his fellow disciples were concerned she was right outside the love of God. But Jesus loved her. It was a love that broke down every prejudice and that was willing to go against cultural norms, to risk criticism, to stop at nothing, to forgive anything (Jn. 4:4-42). That's how God loves you; and that's how he calls you to love others: those we're the least likely to love, those we find it impossible to love, those outside his kingdom.

- *On the road to Jerusalem.* He was young, he was rich, he was in a position of leadership and authority. What's more, he was a good living guy, who wanted what Jesus could give. And 'Jesus looked at him and loved him.' I suppose it could have been because he was a good guy. Or because he wanted to know about eternal life. Or because of the potential that was in him. More likely, Jesus loved him because he loved him. What a moment! A door opening in heaven, the love of God reaching out almost tangibly to this man. But the rich young man turned away, unwilling to pay the price of following Jesus (Mk. 10:17-22). There's never any problem with the love of God; any blockage has got to lie in us.

- *In Bethany.* There was a place Jesus loved to be. It was the home of Martha, Mary and Lazarus in the village of Bethany, just outside of Jerusalem. Perhaps the food was good, perhaps the atmosphere was welcoming, perhaps the place was comfortable and relaxing.

Anyhow, 'Jesus loved Martha and her sister and Lazarus' (Jn. 11:5). And this time his love was welcomed and reciprocated. Their home was Jesus' home. They loved to have him there, and he loved to be there. Even before he had spoken the words, they knew the truth of John 14:23, 'If anyone loves me, he will obey my teaching. My Father will love him, and we will come to him and make our home with him.'

- *In the upper room.* Stressed, weary, hot and smelly, arguing among themselves as to who was the greatest. Hardly a lovable bunch as they met for the Passover meal on the night Jesus was betrayed. But, unbelievably, Jesus knelt before them, and, one by one, washed their feet, even the feet of Judas. Never could John forget that moment; never could he forget the words, 'I have set you an example that you should do as I have done for you.... A new commandment I give you: Love one another. As I have loved you, so you must love one another. By this all men will know that you are my disciples, if you love one another' (Jn. 13:15, 34-35). On that night of all nights he would have shown incredible love if he had just washed the feet of the good guys; but Jesus knelt and washed Judas' feet. Talking about his love for the man who betrayed him to death would have been pretty amazing. But to put that love into practice in such a way; to make it more comfortable for Judas to hurry through the dark streets and sell him to his enemies for thirty silver pieces – that's the astonishing measure of his love. And still we hear those words, 'As I have loved, so you must love.'

- *As Jesus prepares to go to Gethsemane.* When Jesus was preparing to leave the upper room for Gethsemane

(Jn. 14:31) we might expect his mind to be full of the suffering he was to face in the next few hours. But instead the focus of his thoughts was that deep relationship of love he offers to each of his followers. 'As the Father has loved me, so have I loved you. Now remain in my love' (Jn. 15:9). The love is his; it is ours to live in it. To enjoy it. To soak it up. To respond to it. To draw life and strength from it as the branch draws life from the vine. To live it and bear its fruit. To stick with it. To grow in it.

• *On a dark Friday near Jerusalem*. While the rest of the disciples ran away and hid, John stood near the cross and watched the One he loved suffer and die. He heard those amazing words as the soldiers nailed him to the cross, 'Father, forgive them, for they do not know what they are doing' (Lk. 23:34). He saw the way Jesus' love went out, even in those hours of agony, to such contrasting people as his mother and the criminal who was crucified with him (Jn. 19:26-27; Lk. 23:42-43). He witnessed the darkness and the earthquake, the natural world itself trembling at what was happening. And, though as yet he didn't fully understand the meaning of it all, he saw love, the love of God giving his Son as an 'atoning sacrifice for our sins' (1 Jn. 2:2).

'It is finished!' Love has paid the price; love, 'vast as the ocean' has broken the hold of sin. Love that stopped short of nothing, that will stop short of nothing. 'He who did not spare his own Son, but gave him up for us all – how will he not also, along with him, graciously give us all things?' (Rom. 8:32). This is the love of God for you.

*Great God of love, I believe that you love me.
There's a door open in heaven and your love is
pouring out upon me. Forgive me that I've been so
slow to receive and to trust your love. By your
grace I open my whole being to your love, the love
of my Father in heaven, the love of my Saviour:
strong love, holy love, unfailing love. From this
day on may I live in your love.*

14.

Jonah and the compassionate God

Forget the fish for the moment. The real sting of the story of Jonah is in the tail. A sulky prophet sitting on the edge of Nineveh, waiting for God to destroy it (Jon. 4:1,5). After all, it was a pagan city, an evil city, whose rulers had attacked and oppressed the Jews, and God was a just God. What's more, Jonah had prophesied destruction, and no-one enjoys being a false prophet.

Meanwhile, God was seeing things differently. Of course he hated the sin of the people of Nineveh. But he didn't hate the people. In fact he loved them. That was why, with some help from the fish, he got Jonah there, so that they would know how he felt about their sin. And when they knew how God felt about their sin, they felt the same way. Urged on by the king they turned from their sin, and called urgently on God, in the hope that he would 'relent and with compassion turn from his fierce anger' and not destroy them. And when 'God saw what they did and how they turned from their evil ways, he had compassion and did not bring upon them the destruction he had threatened' (Jon. 3:9,10).

In fact this came as no surprise to Jonah, and he tried to tell God that it was this that lay behind the whole fish incident. 'O LORD, is this not what I said when I was still at home? That is why I was so quick to flee to Tarshish. I knew that you are a gracious and compassionate God, slow to anger and abounding in love, a God who relents from sending calamity' (Jon. 4:2). And now his prophetic image was in tatters. 'Now, O LORD, take away my life, for it is better for me to die than to live' (Jon. 4:3).

It seems as though Jonah didn't want God to be compassionate – at any rate not to the Ninevites. That's why God gave him the object lesson of the vine. Jonah liked the vine; it gave him shelter. But then a worm chewed through it and it died, making Jonah thoroughly upset. 'If you can be concerned about a vine,' said God, 'that comes up in a night and dies in a night, why shouldn't I be concerned for the 120,000 people in the great city of Nineveh who don't know their right hand from their left, not to mention lots of dumb animals?'

I rather like that bit about the dumb animals. It's the last phrase of the book in the Hebrew, so it comes with a bit of a punch. Jonah was upset at the destruction of a plant; God was upset at the destruction of 120,000 men and women made in his image. It's as though God is saying to Jonah, 'If you can't feel concerned for the people, at least feel concerned for the cows and the sheep.'

Jonah is an amazing book. Not because of the fish, but because of what it tells us about God. Jonah was a good man, a holy man, God's chosen prophet. He knew God was a good God, a holy God, who hated evil and was committed to judging and destroying it. And he knew about compassion, at least for plants and animals. But in no way could he accept the amazing scope of God's compassion.

Jonah knew his Bible. He knew that on Mount Sinai God proclaimed to Moses his name, the LORD:

'The LORD, the LORD, the compassionate and gracious God, slow to anger, abounding in love and faithfulness, maintaining love to thousands, and forgiving wickedness, rebellion and sin. Yet he does not leave the guilty unpunished; he punishes the children and their children for the sin of the fathers to the third and fourth generations.' (Ex. 34:6-7)

But he couldn't see how the first part of that passage tied in with the second. If God punished sin, how could he be compassionate and forgive it? How could he be true to his holy and just nature, and show compassion at the same time? Indeed, Jonah had a shrewd suspicion of what we are even more sure of, that the repentance of the Ninevites was in fact a pretty limited thing. However genuine it may have been at the time, there's no historical evidence of a lasting change of heart; as far as we know the city didn't give up its pagan gods and start following the God of the Jews, not did it become a paragon of virtue or holiness. So, Jonah might ask, what's the point? Why waste compassion on them?

God's answer was stark. He had given it to Moses centuries before, and Jonah ought to have grasped it: 'I will have mercy on whom I will have mercy, and I will have compassion on whom I will have compassion' (Ex. 33:19). And that's that. He's a God of compassion. He has far more compassion than the most holy and compassionate of humans. He has compassion on those who are wicked; he has compassion on the enemies of his people. Remember how Jesus wept over the city that was about to reject and crucify him?

Be sure of this: you'll never be as compassionate as God. We may not be as tough as Jonah, but all of us need to work at learning the lesson God taught him. Here are a few things God says to me and you today.

1. *Don't judge.* Of course it's right to be discerning over sin, to be clear about what is right and what is wrong. But that doesn't give us the right to be judgmental about people, something expressly forbidden by Jesus (Mt. 7:1). Only God knows the full facts; only he can judge. So practise making allowances, being compassionate. Leave it to non-Christians to criticise, to condemn, to put people down. Don't go along with them; be different; be like Jesus (Jn. 12:47).

2. *Be compassionate towards other Christians.* Christians have often been more gracious and compassionate towards non-Christians than towards their fellow Christians. We've been quick to condemn those who belong to other denominations or whose theology or church practice is different from ours. But if barking like dogs or baptizing babies or believing in a premillennial post-tribulation rapture isn't your scene, don't fall into the trap of condemning and criticising those who are into these things. Save your energies for something better; indeed, pour them into loving your fellow Christians as much as Jesus loves them, even when they're barking and baptizing. Make allowances for them, be gracious towards them, practise compassion towards them. If they need sorting out you can safely leave it to God to do the necessary (Acts 5:38-39).

3. *Be compassionate towards Christians who fail.* Remember Peter and David. Of course there are times when clear action has to be taken; an elder who falls into serious sin should step down from office; someone who

breaks the child protection code should be banned from working with children; someone who refuses to repent of their sin should be disciplined. But even so, such action should still be taken in a spirit of compassion, and every opportunity seized to show the compassion of God towards the offender (see 1 Cor. 5:1-5; 2 Cor. 2:5-11).

4. *Be compassionate towards those who are not yet Christians.* That's the message of the book of Jonah for us today. There's no-one outside the compassion of God. God calls us to share the good news of his love and grace in Jesus with everyone we can reach. So in no way should we do a Jonah and refuse to let them know the gospel. Take on board again that graphic picture in Matthew 9:36–10:10, and apply it to your street, your place of work, your city, your circle of friends, the people you see on your TV. When Jesus sees them he has compassion on them, because they're stressed and driven, caught up in the meaninglessness and emptiness of a godless life, powerless in the face of the pressures and evils of our age. So he says to us, 'There's a big harvest there waiting to be reaped. Get on your knees and ask God to send workers into the harvest field. And, for a start, you go. You tell them the good news; take them healing and life. You've received freely; then give as freely as you have received.'

5. *Work at showing special compassion for the really bad people.* We generally find it easy to be gracious and compassionate towards people who are more or less like us, but often have big hang-ups over paedophiles, bombers, noisy neighbours, bad drivers, Satanists and football hooligans. Jesus was absolutely clear: we

are to love these people (Mt. 5:43-48), and one of the
first stages on the road to loving them is to feel compassion towards them.

6. *Make compassion an attitude and an action, not just a feeling.* Remember the story of the Good Samaritan? I
   doubt that the Samaritan was overcome with love
   and compassion when he saw the wounded Jew. If
   anything his ingrained feelings of hatred and rejection would have risen to the surface. But he showed
   compassion by his attitude and actions. If you find it
   hard to feel compassion for someone, still go ahead
   and adopt a compassionate attitude: refuse to judge
   or condemn; make allowances. Then, whenever you
   can, do something that expresses compassion; be a
   Good Samaritan. To show compassion in action when
   you don't feel compassionate is a particularly beautiful thing to do.

7. *Don't worry over God's compassion.* Different people
   have different problems over God's compassion.
   Some have the Jonah problem, and are afraid God
   may be going soft on sin if he shows compassion to
   sinners. Others have the opposite problem, and are
   afraid of those passages in the Bible which speak of
   God's righteous judgment. 'How can a God of love
   send people to hell?' they ask. 'Why does he let innocent people suffer?' These are big questions, and
   though there are many big answers to them our
   minds are often too small to take in the huge implications of God's nature and purposes. But, whatever
   your particular problem, remember that the compassion of God is big enough to cover every situation,
   and he has no problems at all reconciling it with his
   holiness and justice and righteous judgment. He's

made it clear that he is a gloriously compassionate God; we can safely leave the exercise of that compassion to him.

*For the compassion you've shown towards me
I thank you Lord; I've certainly needed it, and
it's been new every morning. Please go on
giving me your heart, so that in every part of
my life I may express towards others the
compassion you have expressed towards me.*

15.

Ezekiel and the God who comes

In the world of the Old Testament each nation had its own particular god or, more often, gods. Their responsibility was to take care of the nation, to make sure its crops grew, its animals were fertile, and its enemies defeated. In return the people offered worship, prayers, offerings, and a degree of loyalty. Only a degree; it was by no means unheard of for people to get tired of their gods; someone else's gods seemed more exciting; the worship, perhaps, was more orgiastic, or the sexual experiences available at the temple were more attractive.

There was another reason for changing your gods. If two nations were about to go to war, each nation, naturally, would pray to its gods for victory. Then they would fight: one side would win and the other would lose. The losers would then be enslaved or made tributary by the winners, often, in effect, being incorporated into their nation. By a simple bit of logic it would have been clear to both sides that the gods of the winners were better at hearing prayer and helping their devotees than those of the losers. So, besides being absorbed generally into the conquering nation, it would seem reasonable to the losers to take over the winners' gods as well.

That was the pressure faced by the Jews when they were defeated by the Babylonians in 597 BC. It was especially strong on those who were taken captive by Nebuchadnezzar and settled in Babylonia. Indeed, there was an extra pressure on them. It was common to think of the gods of various nations as local to that nation. That is, the gods of the Babylonians ruled over Babylonia and exercised plenty of power there. But Sicily or Spain were outside their territory, so in those countries Sicilian or Spanish gods were in charge.

It may have been this kind of thinking that made Jonah think that by getting a ship to Spain he could get outside the influence of God's authority. So the exiles in Babylon, surrounded by the often huge representations of the Babylonian deities, feeling that their God was 500 miles away, broken and defeated in Jerusalem, would have felt the pressure to give up trusting in God. They had lost the battle, their city, their loved ones, their freedom, and their God. No wonder they sat down by the waters of Babylon and wept.

Among them was Ezekiel, a young man who was called by God to be a prophet among the exiles, even though, as God told him right at the start, few of them would accept his prophecies. One day, five years into the exile, he had a spectacular experience of meeting God, which he describes in graphic detail in Ezekiel 1. Out of the north (the direction from which a traveller would arrive from Jerusalem) came a magnificent storm, with wind and cloud and lightening. In the heart of the storm were four mighty angelic beings carrying nothing less than the throne of God. On the throne Ezekiel saw with his own eyes a figure 'like that of a man', burning with fire and brilliant light and surrounded with radiant glory. 'This', he wrote, 'was the appearance of the likeness of the glory of the LORD. When I saw it, I fell face down, and I heard the voice of one speaking' (Ezek. 1:28).

People have spent lots of time and energy puzzling over the fine details of Ezekiel 1. But God hasn't put this chapter in our Bibles to encourage us to speculate about flying saucers or the like. It's there to describe Ezekiel's encounter with God, and, in doing that to teach us more about the God whom we too can meet.

- *The God who comes.* God knew how the exiles felt; he knew they were tempted to think that he was 500 miles away in Jerusalem. So he chose to come to them, in power and glory, speeding across the desert, giving them a graphic demonstration that they were not alone, they were not cut off from him by the distance. He was with them in Babylonia just as much as he was in Jerusalem. Of course, in a general sense, God was already there since he's everywhere; but he came in this special way to encourage and strengthen them in their need. That's our God! He's the God who comes. All through the Bible, in all sorts of ways, God has come, to patriarchs and kings, to ordinary people like Hagar, to Solomon and the people as they dedicated the temple, to prophets as he called them, to Zechariah and Mary at the beginning of the gospel story. Each coming is different, through an angel, through a vision or a dream, in glory or in a still small voice. And the climax of it all was at Bethlehem, when God came in Jesus. Our God is the God who comes.

- *The God who comes in fire.* Phrases like 'flashing lightning', 'fire', 'burning coals' and 'torches' come all through Ezekiel's description of his meeting with God. Others, too, experienced the fire of God, such as the Israelites at Mount Sinai, and Elijah on Mount

Carmel. But the supreme coming of God in 'tongues of fire' was at Pentecost, when God came to his people, and so to us, in the Holy Spirit (Acts 2:3). Fire speaks of holiness, the burning purity of our great God. It speaks of judgment, the destruction of all that is evil. It speaks of passion, supremely the passionate fire of God's love, but also the fire of his anger against sin and evil, and his passionate commitment to righteousness and goodness. This is the fire that God has put into our hearts by his Holy Spirit. Take care lest you put it out (1 Thes. 5:19); work at fanning it into a blaze (2 Tim. 1:6).

• *The God who comes with life.* The exiles may well have thought that God was lying half-dead back in Jerusalem. But when he came to Ezekiel, he made it abundantly clear that he was still what he had always been, the living God. One of the features of Ezekiel's vision is movement; the living creatures that bear his throne 'sped back and forth like flashes of lightning' (Ezek. 1:14); the throne is carried on 'wheels' which could go in any direction, including upwards, and were constantly on the move (Ezek. 1:15-21). No tired, idle God, this. Rather, a God who is full of life, full of energy, on the move. And this is the life that he brings to his weak and dispirited people.

• *The God who comes with power.* When I read Ezekiel 1 my thoughts often go back to when, as a small boy, I would stand next to a mighty steam locomotive waiting at Bristol Temple Meads to take an express train up to the North of England. The first few miles were a steep climb, and the fire would have been stoked up to white heat to produce maximum steam. As the engine waited, raring to go, the steam pressure would build up and up until the safety valve released it with a roar that made us cover our ears and run. Pent up power – that's our God. Power to do the impossible, the amazing; power for his people when the Holy Spirit comes on them (Acts 1:8); power to pull down the strongholds of evil (2 Cor. 10:4), to bring in the kingdom of God. Rightly, we may be conscious of our weakness, and our inability to do anything effective apart from him (Jn. 15:5). But the fact is we are on the top of a volcano, packed with the energy and power of the living God, ready at the right moment to be released to accomplish great things for his kingdom (Jn. 14:12).

• *The God who comes with glory.* Ezekiel saw 'the glory of the LORD' (Ezek. 3:23); and he saw it not just once but again and again. When God came he came in glory, in brilliant light, in majesty. 'Like the appearance of a rainbow in the clouds on a rainy day, so was the radiance around him. This was the appearance of the likeness of the glory of the LORD' (Ezek. 1:28). When God came in Jesus his glory was for the most part veiled, but it was there for those with eyes to see and hearts to receive it. As we have seen with Moses, it is ours to be hungry for his glory, both that we might glimpse it, and that others around us may see it too. These are days in which we need to pray that 'the glory of the LORD will be revealed, and all mankind together will see it' (Is. 40:5).

• *The God who comes and equips.* God came to his people in exile not just to be with them, but to do things, to work out his purposes in and through them. In particular he came to Ezekiel to equip him to be a prophet and to give him the message the people needed to hear. He knew that Ezekiel's task was a tough one, so he gave him the visions of his power and nearness, and, often in graphic and practical ways, he gave him the message he had been called to deliver. Through the Holy Spirit God comes to us and equips us for the tasks he has for us (Jn. 14:16-18), giving us what we need to go in his name and share his truth with the world around us.

- *The God who comes to you now.* It may be in power and great glory; it may be in a 'gentle whisper' (1 Kgs. 19:12). He may come to encourage; he may come to sort you out where you've gone wrong. God still loves to come to his people. He stands at the door and knocks; he comes near to us as we come near to him; he promises that as we seek we will find (Rev. 3:20; Jas. 4:8; Mt. 7:7-8). So take time now to meet with him. Invite him to come in with his life, to reinvigorate you, to lift you up and set you on your feet, to encourage and envision you. Ask him to come with his fire, to burn out what is evil, to set your heart on fire again with his love and passion for those around you and for the coming of his kingdom in a hurting and lost world. Invite him to come and show his glory, both to you and through you to others. And ask him to come in power; to fill you with his Spirit, to equip you to serve, to give you words that are powerful, a message that is effective and life-changing, so that his kingdom comes and his will is done on earth as in heaven.

Come, Mighty God. Come, Emmanuel. Come, Spirit of the living God. Come to me, as I draw near to you. Come in fire and life and power and glory, or in a gentle whisper. Come as you choose, but come. And not just to me, but to all your people; in our weakness and need we cry to you, 'Come.'

16.

Pentecost and the God who fills with his fullness

There's a mind-blowing prayer in Ephesians chapter 3. Paul has been writing about the amazing purposes of God, that the Gentiles as well as the Jews are 'a dwelling in which God lives by his Spirit' (Eph. 2:22). It's because of this, he says, he prays for the Christians at Ephesus that through the power of the Spirit Christ may truly make his home in their hearts and lives, that they 'may be filled to the measure of all the fulness of God' (Eph. 3:19).

That's impossible! It's pretty amazing that God comes to us at all. It's even more amazing that he comes to make his home in us. Maybe it's understandable that, since he is very very big, if he comes into us he'll take up a lot of room. And perhaps we may be willing to clear out all the junk so that he can actually take up all the room and fill us with himself. But then to go on and pray that he'll fill us 'to the measure of all the fulness of God' is surely over the top. It's like praying for all the vastness of the universe to be packed into a pinhead.

Hmm... That's a thought. If the scientists are right, some fifteen billion years ago our great God did just that – packed the whole universe into a space smaller than a pinhead. If he could do that, perhaps we ought to be careful about using the word 'impossible' when talking about any of his actions. Maybe what's mind blowingly impossible to us is still somehow possible to him (Lk. 1:37). After all, Paul does follow that prayer for the fullness of God with a description of God as someone 'who is able to do immeasurably more than all we ask or imagine' (Eph. 3:20).

So there's got to be something here for each of us, and for the church of Jesus Christ as a whole. God wants us to be full, and he wants us to be full with his fullness. Whether we understand what that means or not, whether we think we'll ever get that full or not, here's something that God offers to us that we need to receive.

'There's a huge task in front of you,' said Jesus to his disciples, 'to bring the good news to the whole world. Just as my Father sent me, I'm sending you. But don't go until the Father fulfils his promise that he will come to you through the Holy Spirit, to fill you and empower you for all that lies ahead.' So the disciples waited, and on the Day of Pentecost God came in his fullness; the promise was fulfilled, to 'pour out my Spirit on all people' (Acts 2:17). He came in wind and fire, and 'all of them were filled with the Holy Spirit' (Acts 2:4).

Pentecost was a special occasion, but it wasn't the only time the people of God had the experience of being filled with the Holy Spirit. We all need a regular topping up – and sometimes major refills – since we so easily allow other things to push God out of the central position in our lives. Often, too, we need a fresh in-filling to face a particularly tough situation or fulfil a specific call from God.

Shortly after Pentecost, when the new group of believers at Jerusalem was beginning to face serious opposition from the Jewish authorities, the place where they were meeting for prayer was shaken. And 'they were all filled with the Holy Spirit and spoke the word of God boldly. All the believers were one in heart and mind. No-one claimed that any of his possessions was his own, but they shared everything they had. With great power the apostles continued to testify to the resurrection of the Lord Jesus, and much grace was upon them all' (Acts 4:31-33).

What a picture of a God-filled community of Christian believers. Despite the opposition, they were overflowing with bold witness, bubbling over with practical love, and anointed with grace, 'much grace', just as Jesus himself was 'full of grace' (Jn. 1:14).

Sadly, there's been controversy over some of the details of what it means to be filled with God through his Spirit. Perhaps that's not surprising since this is something so big that none of us will ever be able to understand it wholly. But, whatever you do, don't let the problems or controversial issues stop you from experiencing and living the reality that the Bible talks about. God comes to us; he comes as the triune God, in Christ, through the Holy Spirit. He comes in his fullness, and it is his intention that we should be filled 'to the measure of all the fulness of God.' That's something he wants for everyone of us, including you; so leave aside the difficult details and the controversies and go for the real thing. Join that group of believers meeting together early on the Day of Pentecost, seeking God in prayer, open to his coming, hungry for his fullness.

- *Be filled – receive the gift of his fullness.* 'In Christ,' wrote Paul to the Colossians, 'all the fulness of the Deity lives in bodily form, and you have been given fulness in Christ' (Col. 2:9-10). Fullness, like salvation, isn't something we have to earn. If it was, none of us would ever get anywhere near it. It is a gift. The Colossian Christians, like all churches, were a mixed lot, and none of them had been Christians for long; but Paul had no problem stating categorically that they had all been given God's fullness in Christ. What was true for them is true of you and me. God has given; it is ours to receive.

- *Be filled – so there's no room for nasties.* Paul follows up his prayer for the fullness of God in Ephesians 3 by writing about the work of the Spirit in the people of God, uniting and gifting and maturing them, 'so that the body of Christ may be built up... attaining to the whole measure of the fulness of Christ' (Eph. 4:12,13). Later on he warns against grieving the Holy Spirit by hanging on to our old way of living, instead of letting Christ live in us (Eph. 4:17-5:21). Instead of the old nasties, like deceit, anger, theft, 'unwholesome talk', sexual immorality, impurity, greed, obscenity, and 'coarse joking', we must be filled up with Christ – so full that there's no room left for the nasties. 'Do not get drunk on wine, which leads to debauchery. Instead, be filled with the Spirit' (Eph. 5:18). There's the choice. We can be filled up with alcohol, or filled up with the Spirit. We can be full of nasties, or full of Christ.

- *Be filled – the great God living in you.* 'This is what was spoken by the prophet Joel,' said Peter to the crowds on the Day of Pentecost. 'In the last days, God says, I will pour out my Spirit on all people' (Acts 2:17). 'If anyone loves me,' said Jesus, 'he will obey my teaching. My

Father will love him, and we will come to him and make our home with him' (Jn. 14:23). In the Old Testament days the indwelling presence of God was limited to a privileged few. Now the gift is open to all; God comes in his fullness to all his children without distinction (Acts 2:17-18). 'All of them were filled with the Holy Spirit' (Acts 2:4). No-one missed out on it; make sure you don't.

• *Be filled – the great God living in your church.* Think what a difference it would make to so many of our churches if they were really filled with the living God. What grace and power there would be among us, what reality in our worship, what vibrancy in our witness and service. Paul pictures an unbeliever coming to such a church: 'He will fall down and worship God, exclaiming, "God is really among you!"' (1 Cor. 14:25). That's how God wants it to be. Not churches that have lost their first love; not churches that are lukewarm; but churches that will open the door and let him in with all his grace and fullness (Rev. 2:4, 3:15-20). Pray for this, for your church and for all churches; maybe this is the greatest need of our churches today.

• *Be filled – so that you overflow.* 'Jesus stood and said in a loud voice, "If anyone is thirsty, let him come to me and drink. Whoever believes in me, as the Scripture has said, streams of living water will flow from within him." By this he meant the Spirit, whom those who believed in him were later to receive' (Jn. 7:37-39). God comes to us in his fullness; he fills us with himself; he lives in our lives and in the communities of our churches. But there's so much of him, he's bound to overflow. His goodness is so great that it's bound to be expressed in our good deeds. His joy is so rich that it's bound to set our lives singing. His peace is so deep, it's got to flow from us to those around us. Our lives must reflect his love and grace. His truth must be expressed by what we are and what we say. And it's not to be just a trickle of these things, a drop here and a bit there. It's to be a stream, a river like the one Ezekiel described coming from the temple of God – small to start with, but soon becoming knee deep and then a mighty river, waters to swim in, too deep to cross. Wherever that river goes it brings life; trees grow abundantly on its banks, filled with fruit and clothed with leaves that bring healing. Its waters teem with life; so full of life is it that when its waters enter the Dead Sea, the poisoned waters there too are transformed and teem with life (Ezek. 47:1-12). That is God's vision and calling for you, as your life is filled with his fullness and overflows to those around you.

Yes, Lord, that's what I need; that's what I want. You in your fullness: filling, purifying, overwhelming my life, overflowing to those around. And, again, Lord, not just me: please, my local church, all your people – we need you so desperately. Fill us to overflowing with yourself so that we may truly be the people of God.

17.

Samuel and the God who speaks

One of the greatest contrasts between the God of the Bible and the other gods of the day was that the other gods were dumb. 'Mute idols', Paul called them (1 Cor. 12:2). 'They have mouths, but cannot speak... nor can they utter a sound with their throats,' mocked the psalmist (Ps. 115:5,7). God, on the other hand, is far from dumb; he is a God who speaks.

In Genesis 1 he spoke words of power that brought the universe into being. To Abraham he spoke words of promise. To his people he spoke words of command and instruction. Through the prophets he spoke rebuke, and shared his unfolding purposes.

In the New Testament he spoke supremely in Jesus, the Word. 'In the past God spoke to our forefathers through the prophets in many times and in various ways, but in these last days he has spoken to us by his Son' (Heb. 1:1-2). Through the apostles and the writings of the New Testament God continued to speak; by the Holy Spirit he still speaks to those who are ready to hear his voice. Our God is the God who speaks.

Three thousand years ago God spoke to a boy who was a helper in the building that had taken the place of God's tent of meeting at Shiloh. The boy, Samuel, didn't realize it was God speaking to him, and needed the wisdom of Eli the priest. 'If he calls you, say, "Speak, LORD, for your servant is listening"' (1 Sam. 3:9). He did as he was told, and God spoke again, and then on many other occasions. 'The LORD continued to appear at Shiloh, and there he revealed himself to Samuel through his word' (1 Sam. 3:21).

God hasn't given up on speaking. He's still doing it, in dozens of ways. Sometimes he speaks with an audible voice, as he did to Saul of Tarsus on the road to Damascus. Often he speaks in the stillness of the human heart, or through a preacher or a book or a Christian friend. Sometimes his word comes in a distinctive way, as a word of prophecy or of wisdom; sometimes it is not even verbalized, but comes as an awareness of his nearness or his truth or his goodness. Key to his speaking are two things: the Bible and the Holy Spirit.

The Bible is a rich record of what God has said to many people in all sorts of situations down through the centuries. More than that, it's his word to us today, as relevant now as it was when it was first written. The Holy Spirit speaks his word to our hearts, taking the words of the Bible and applying them to us, or speaking to us through a situation, an experience, a preacher, and so on.

Has God spoken to you lately? I'm pretty certain he has; after all, no decent parent is going to go for long without speaking to her or his child. If you feel that he hasn't spoken to you recently, the problem's got to be with your listening, not with his speaking. So maybe you ought to join Samuel, young and naive, but willing to hear the voice of the true God: 'Speak, Lord, for your servant is listening.'

- *Ask God to speak.* He'll speak sooner or later whether you ask him or not. But if you start by asking him, you'll be putting yourself in the right place before him. 'Speak, Lord, for your servant is listening' is a tuning in, switching on the phone. 'I'm listening, Lord. I'm ready to hear you speak.'

- *Expect God to speak.* God's surely got something to say about your work situation, the way that relationship has developed, the tasks he's setting before you, the meaning of last Wednesday's Bible study for your life, the way you drive your car, and a thousand other things. And then there are the words of encouragement he wants to speak, and truths about himself he wants to reveal. He's got so much to say. Listen, and expect to hear.

- *Work hard at listening.* We come away from the Sunday service as empty as when we went. 'I didn't get anything out of that. God didn't say anything to me.' And yet the Bible was read, worship songs were sung, the sermon was preached, perhaps you took bread and wine, you talked with godly men and women. Could it be that all that time God was silent? Granted, the Bible reader made a mess of the pronunciation and the phrasing, but it was the word of God; didn't he say anything? The worship may have been heavy and the band out of tune, but were there no profound truths in the words? Didn't God whisper, 'I love you', or 'I forgive you'? Yes, it was a pretty poor sermon, but was it so bad that God didn't get one word in edge ways? When it comes to hearing God's voice we're all pretty bad listeners. We need to train ourselves to shut out all the other voices that clamour for our attention, to pray Samuel's prayer, and then give God space and time to speak.

- *Let God speak the way he chooses*. In the Bible he spoke through dreams, a talking ass, a burning bush, angels, prophecy, a still small voice, a storm, individuals, circumstances, visions, letters, and many other ways. We may have our preferences about the way we'd like him to speak to us, but the choice has to be left with him. Be careful you don't miss what he's saying because he says it in a way you weren't expecting. Don't, for example, insist on getting a word of prophecy, when God has already spoken on the issue in the Bible or through a wise Christian friend.

- *Make full use of the Bible*. There's no shortage of God's words there! Always approach the Bible recognizing it as God's Word and with a prayer that the Holy Spirit will enable you to understand and receive it. If you find you get bogged down in some part of the Bible leave it aside and focus on parts that you find clear and helpful. You can return later to the difficult passage using a book or a commentary to help you understand it; but so much of the Bible is clear and straightforward that it's wise to listen for God's voice where he's speaking plainly. Focus especially on Jesus, who is the key to the whole of the Bible. As you read expect God to speak to you both generally and specifically. He speaks generally when, for example, you read Paul's instructions on how to live a holy life; this is God's Word for all his people, and so for you. But at times as you read a Bible passage the Holy Spirit will say something specific and personal to you. It may be, for example, that you are reading a passage which talks about reconciliation, and as you read it the Holy Spirit tells you to take specific steps to repair a damaged relationship.

- *Listen with others.* God doesn't just speak to individuals; often he speaks to a group of his people. He directs a local church to engage in a specific evangelistic programme; he calls all his people to make poverty history. Some of the richest times of hearing God's voice that I've experienced have been when I've met with a group of Christians for a day of prayer over some specific issue. At the start of the day we all had different thoughts and ideas; at the end we were one in heart and mind, knowing that God had spoken to us all. Study the Bible and pray together with a Christian friend or in a small group, and share together what God is saying.

- *Develop the art of listening to sermons.* Preaching is an art, but so is listening to a sermon. Don't make the mistake of leaving the preacher to do all the work. The sermon isn't meant to be the part of the service where you settle back and expect to be entertained (or bored). Come to the sermon expectant. Pray that God will speak and that you will hear clearly. Keep your mind and heart engaged; don't slip into neutral or drift off on some tangent. Ask questions: 'What does this mean for me?', 'How does that verse apply in my situation?' Be ready for God's voice; 'Speak, Lord, for your servant is listening.'

- *Check what you hear.* God always speaks infallibly, but we never hear infallibly. There's always a degree of distortion; we get most of the message but miss some of it; we hear what God is saying, but interpret it to fit in with our way of seeing things. Sometimes we mistake other voices for the voice of God. We all know of instances where people have claimed to have heard God telling them this or that and it's pretty clear that it's just their imagination or they're twisting God's Word to suit their own ends. So we always need to check what we are hearing, to make sure we've got it right. The Bible, and particularly the teaching of Jesus, is key here. God will never say something to us that contradicts what he has already said in the Bible. Since people have sometimes used the Bible wrongly – for example they've used some bloodthirsty passage in the Old Testament to say that God is telling them to go and slaughter their enemies – we need to check carefully that we are using the Bible rightly, keeping Jesus as the key to our understanding and interpretation. Another good gift God has given us in this context is wise Christian friends. We can share with them what we feel God is saying and listen to their response. They won't be infallible, but God may use them to modify what we've heard, or to help us understand and apply it more correctly.

- *Be ready for surprises*. When Jesus spoke, the people were shocked. Instead of saying what they expected to hear, so often he seemed to say the opposite: 'Blessed are the poor', 'Love your enemies', 'Be glad when you suffer', 'The least is the greatest in the king-dom of heaven.' When Paul was pressing ahead on an evangelistic tour, the Holy Spirit twice turned him back, and then God spoke through a vision sending him off in an unexpected direction (Acts 16:6-10). Much of what God says to us will be familiar, but sometimes he will surprise us, applying his word in a way we didn't expect, or setting a task before us that we'd never imagined would come our way. So be warned! God is a God of surprises, and he may have some unexpected things to say.

Speak, Lord, for your servant is listening.

18.

Planet earth and the God who judges

We sang that awful hymn in church yesterday.

Which one?

All about God coming with clouds descending to judge the world. The one where you have to sing 'Deeply wailing' three times and 'Come to judgement!' four times over. Clearly the guy who wrote it had never heard of God's love and grace.

I'm not sure you're right there; actually it was Charles Wesley, the man who wrote 'Love Divine'.

Really? Well, give me 'Love Divine' any day; at least that ends up in heaven; 'Lo! He comes' seems to land us all in hell.

No way! It's describing Jesus coming back to set up his kingdom in power and glory.

Then why does it talk about judgement?

Because God's kingdom is perfect; it can't contain any-thing evil. So before it can be finally established every-thing that is evil has got to be destroyed. So God, through Jesus, has got to judge everything to get rid of evil.

So hell is where evil is destroyed?

That's right.

And where innocent people who don't happen to be Christians suffer for ever and ever?

No way. If the Bible's clear on anything, it's clear on the justice of God. If God is anything, he's got to be just and fair. No innocent person will suffer, and no-one will suf-fer anything unfairly.

Where does it say that?

All over the place. But if you want a specific verse or two, how about Psalm 96:13: 'He comes to judge the earth. He will judge the world in righteousness and the people in his truth.' Or Revelation 15:3-4, 'Just and true are your ways... your righteous acts have been revealed.' And you need to remember that the one who'll be doing the judging is Jesus. There's no way he's going to be cruel or mean or unfair.

But what about those bits where it talks about Jesus destroying his enemies? I heard a sermon once on a verse from Revelation, all about people hiding, terrified at the judgement, and calling on the mountains to fall on them and hide them from the face of God and from the wrath of the Lamb. Real bloodthirsty stuff it was; I think the preacher really enjoyed it, but I found it repulsive.

Fair enough; I find bits of Revelation a bit hard to take,
too. But you've got to remember at least three things.
First, Revelation is using pictures to describe judgement
and heaven and hell; we don't have to take it all literally.
Second, the pictures are painted graphically to stir us to
action: to make sure that we're not destined for hell, and
to motivate us to do everything we can so that none of
our friends or the people around us end up there. And,
third, you've got to balance these passages with the rest
of the Bible. When it talks about 'the wrath of the Lamb',
for instance, you've got to set alongside that the story of
Jesus weeping over Jerusalem. No way is his judgement
cruel and vindictive. If he condemns anyone to hell, it's
with tears in his eyes.

*But surely, if that's how he feels, he could have done something
to save people from hell.*

Right. And he did. And not just something. He did
everything. He became man: he suffered; he carried the
sin of the world; he died on the cross. He offers forgiveness and eternal life to anyone who'll receive it. The only
thing he stops short of is forcing people to go to heaven.
If someone is determined to hang on to evil, then, when
he passes judgement on that evil and condemns it to
destruction, he has no option but to judge and condemn
that person along with it. It seems to me God has done
everything he can to save people from the judgement.
Can you think of anything else he might have done?

*Well, he could have made it easier for people to hear the gospel
and become Christians. Then there would be less people in hell.*

Yes, possibly. But you've got to remember that the main
reason people don't hear the gospel and find it easy to

become Christians is us. Jesus told Christians to take the gospel to everyone, and two thousand years later we've still not done it. And sometimes we've made such a mess of being Christians that we've turned people off Christianity. If we had all been the people we should have been, like Jesus himself, and done what God called us to do, surely the whole world would be Christian by now.

So you're saying you can't blame God, because the problem lies with us. But that doesn't seem very fair, either. Couldn't God have done something else, reverted to Plan B, when he found that we were making such a mess of things?

Well, I don't know all the details of God's plans. But I'm pretty sure of one thing, that everyone in the world – even someone who's never heard the gospel – does have a chance of seeking God and finding him. Paul talks about people seeing him through his creation, the world around us; and maybe God in his grace reveals something of who he is specifically to their hearts. I don't know how he does it, but I'm sure that God is clever enough to find some way of being scrupulously fair and just. But that still doesn't take from us the responsibility to tell the good news about Jesus, and to show the truth of it by the way we live.

OK, I can accept that. But let's go back to the Day of Judgement. What's the basis of judgement? From what you were saying a moment ago it's whether or not we want to hold on to evil and sin. Most of the preachers I've heard say that it's whether or not we've accepted Jesus as our Saviour. But then passages like Matthew 25, the bit about the sheep and the goats, seem to say it's on the basis of what we've done or not done. Which is right?

Well, I don't think they really contradict each other, so I suppose they're all right. It's like so many things in the Bible: the theme of judgement is such a big one you can't possibly wrap it up in one neat formula. Instead, you have to take several aspects of it and put them together to form a balanced picture.

But surely there's a contradiction if some say the key issue is faith and some say the key issue is works?

Well, let me put it the way I see it. If you really get down to brass tacks the only thing that's important is our relationship with God. You could say that everyone has two options: life with God or life without God. Since all of us have sinned, and sin separates us from God, in a sense we're all self-condemned to a life without God here on earth and then after we die. But in his mercy and grace God has made it possible for us to turn away from our sin and be forgiven and so have a relationship with him, both now and after we die. Heaven is where God is; those who have a relationship with God will get that relationship gloriously fulfilled in heaven. But those who reject God wouldn't be able to cope with heaven because it's so full of what they don't want. Heaven would be hell for them; they've chosen evil, and evil is what they get: the home of evil, hell. Letting God set us free from sin and evil and accepting Jesus as our Saviour are two sides of the same coin. It's through what Jesus has done that sin is dealt with in our lives.

But what about the sheep and the goats?

Well, I don't think there's any real contradiction there with what I've been saying. The criterion for judgement is what people have done with Jesus; people have encountered Jesus without realizing it in the hungry and the thirsty and the stranger and the ill and the prisoners. And they will be judged according to the way they responded.

So is that saying that if someone's never heard about Jesus but Jesus comes to them in the suffering of others and they respond positively, then that counts as receiving Jesus as their Saviour?

Well, Matthew 25 clearly says that they will be given a place in the kingdom. No-one can get to heaven without having Jesus as their Saviour, so I suppose you have to say that they've received what they have seen of Jesus, and in receiving that they've received the Saviour. It's like the thief on the cross; as far as we know, his theological understanding of who Jesus was and what salvation meant was minimal. But he received what he did see and understand, and in God's book that was enough.

So you're saying that when someone responds positively to what they experience of Jesus in others, even if they've never actually heard of him, if someone then later tells them about Jesus and the cross they'd accept that too?

Yes, definitely. And that's the answer to those who say that if people can get to heaven without actually hearing the gospel then we needn't bother to take the gospel to them. Of course we've got to obey the command to preach the gospel to everyone, even though there are other ways in which people can experience something of God. The gospel is God's full revelation, and that's what everyone needs to hear. In all fairness I ought to add that not everyone agrees with what I've just said about the sheep and the goats. Some believe that if a person doesn't actually hear the gospel there's no possibility of them going to heaven, so they say the 'righteous' in Matthew 25 are those who've already heard and received the gospel and then show it by their good works.

If they're right it's even more important to get on and tell everybody about Jesus.

I'd say that it's an urgent task on either interpretation. Though some issues may be obscure, the Bible's call to get on and tell people the good news is absolutely clear. God wants everyone to be saved and come to a knowledge of the truth. He doesn't want to have to condemn anyone. That's why the Judge went to the cross.

> *These are big issues, Lord, and I thank you that I can trust your wisdom and goodness. You have done so much to save people from hell; help me to be as concerned as you are for those who are lost, and to do everything I can to tell them about Jesus.*

19.

White robes and the God who saves

All through the Bible God is the God who saves. The Jews of the Old Testament saw the Exodus, when God saved his people from captivity and made them his own, as the key event in their history. Jesus came into the world to save sinners, indeed, to save the world (1 Tim. 1:15; Jn. 3:17). We'll take one chapter at the end of the Bible, Revelation 7, to highlight the implications of having a God who saves.

1. *'Salvation belongs to our God.'* That's what they shout about in heaven (Rev. 7:10). We've got a God who saves. We don't save ourselves; there's no way we possibly could save ourselves. By grace we have been saved, through faith; it's not from ourselves, 'it is the gift of God' (Eph. 2:8). Salvation from start to finish is God. In love and mercy he decided to save us. In grace and power he found a way of saving us. On the cross of Calvary he broke the power of sin and evil and set us free. Through the work of the Holy Spirit he brings us to himself, out of darkness into the glorious light of

his presence. By his power he keeps us and leads us on from one degree of glory to another. And, like him, his salvation is eternal; it'll never begin to fade, never grow old.

2. *Salvation is Jesus.* 'Salvation belongs... to the Lamb.' Salvation from start to finish is Jesus. His name means Saviour; 'You are to give him the name Jesus, because he will save his people from their sins' (Mt. 1:21). We're saved because Jesus has saved us. He loved us and gave himself for us. He bore our sins in his body on the cross. He was made sin for us. In him we have redemption, the forgiveness of our sins (Gal. 2:20; 1 Pet. 2:24; 2 Cor. 5:21; Col. 1:14). Salvation is Jesus. To know salvation is to know Jesus. To live salvation is to live Jesus. He is our 'righteousness, holiness and redemption'; so if we're going to boast about anything, boast about him (1 Cor. 1:30-31).

3. *Salvation begins now.* 'Everyone who calls on the name of the Lord will be saved,' said Peter on the Day of Pentecost (Acts 2:21). The full experience of salvation will not be ours until we're in the presence of God in heaven, but already we have redemption. That is, God has made us his. Our sins are forgiven; Jesus has 'freed us from our sins by his blood, and has made us to be a kingdom and priests to serve his God and Father' (Rev. 1:5-6). God has put his indelible mark on us, his 'seal' upon our foreheads (Rev. 7:3). His hand of grace and power in on us, so that the winds of evil cannot destroy us.

4. *Salvation is secure.* People have puzzled over the 144,000 described in Revelation 7:5-8, and how they fit in with the 'great multitude' described in the rest

of the chapter. Some have suggested they are a special group within the great multitude – super-saints, or maybe Jewish believers. Much more likely, the two groups are the same: the 144,000 are the great multitude, only viewed in a different way. To describe the same thing in two contrasting ways is no problem for the book of Revelation; Jesus is described as a Lion and then as a Lamb in consecutive verses (Rev. 5:5-6). In keeping with the symbolism of the book of Revelation, 144,000 (12x1000x12) pictures completeness and security. Even though we are a great multitude, too big for anyone to count, God knows every one of his people; not one of them escapes his attention; every one is known and every one is sealed. We are kept secure, whatever we may have to face here on earth.

5. *Salvation is big.* The vision of the 'great multitude' may be familiar to us, but in the first century it must have been amazing and incredibly encouraging. Though Christianity had begun to spread, the believers were still only a tiny minority in the world, with the powers of evil determined to wipe them out. What's more, they expected the end of the world to come pretty soon. Yet here's a vision of vast numbers of people being saved. Heaven will be big, because salvation is big. Salvation is big, because God is big.

6. *Salvation is worldwide.* Again, for its first century readers the scope of Revelation 7:9 must have been mind blowing. Though their knowledge of world geography may have been limited, they knew there were hundreds and even thousands of remote nations and tribes, as far flung as Britain to the Northwest, China in the East, and Africa to the South, who as yet had

not heard the gospel. Yet God promises that before his throne there will be those from 'every nation, tribe, people and language.' And that must include the tribes that still, two thousand years later, haven't heard the gospel. That's his vision; that's the scope of his salvation.

7. *Salvation includes suffering.* The logic of the New Testament is straightforward. Salvation is Jesus; those who are saved are one with Jesus. Jesus suffered; if we're one with him we too will suffer. 'We are God's children,' wrote Paul, 'heirs of God and co-heirs with Christ, if indeed we share in his sufferings in order that we may also share in his glory' (Rom. 8:17). The great multitude before the throne of God are those 'who have come out of the great tribulation' (Rev. 7:14). The 'great tribulation' is the suffering all God's people go through in 'the last days', the days in which we live now. Jesus referred to it in John 16:33; we're already in the thick of it, and some think it will grow worse as the end of the age approaches. It takes many forms; we in the West don't suffer the persecution that Christians in other parts of the world have to go through; but we can be sure that the powers of evil will find lots of ways to make our lives tough, and that Jesus will give us all sorts of opportunities of taking up our cross and following him (Mt. 10:38). One day, of course, our salvation will be complete, and all suffering will be over (Rev. 7:16); but in the meantime, salvation includes suffering.

8. *Salvation means white robes.* There's a lovely balance both in Revelation 7 and 19, which helps us understand the relationship between salvation as a gift and a lifestyle. God's saved people wear 'white

robes' made of 'fine linen, bright and clean' which have been given to them by God (Rev. 19:8). These robes are also 'the righteous acts of the saints'; they are robes that the wearers have washed 'in the blood of the Lamb' to make them white (Rev. 19:8, 7:14). In the first century, as new Christians were baptized and came out of the water they were given white robes which symbolized two things: the gift of salvation which they had received, and the new life which they were about to live, a holy and pure and Christlike life. Salvation, pictured in Revelation 7 and 19 by the white robes and clean linen, is God's gift: the robes can only be white because of the shed blood of Jesus on the cross. But salvation must show; it must be expressed in our lives; so the white robes are equally 'the righteous acts of the saints.' We have the responsibility to wash our robes, and, through the blood of Jesus, make sure they are white. God in his love and grace allows us to be involved in the way his salvation works itself out; by his Spirit we live it and show it through our white robes. 'Work out your salvation with fear and trembling,' wrote Paul to the Philippians, 'for it is God who works in you to will and to act according to his good purpose' (Phil. 2:12-13).

9. *Salvation is the presence of God*. Sometimes we think of salvation mainly in terms of what we are saved from: from sin, from the power of evil, from hell. But the great climax of Revelation 7 makes it clear that the thing that really matters is what, or rather who we're saved to.

> 'They are before the throne of God
> and serve him day and night in his temple;

and he who sits on the throne will spread his tent over them.

For the Lamb at the centre of the throne will be their shepherd;

   he will lead them to springs of living water.

And God will wipe away every tear from their eyes.' (Rev. 7:15,17)

We are saved so that we can be in the presence of God – so we can see him and know him, worship and serve him. We are saved so that he can 'spread his tent' over us. In a sense this is the other side of the coin from that great verse which speaks of the Father and Jesus coming to make their home in our lives (Jn. 14:23); here God is drawing us into his home; he's spreading the tent of his presence, his joy, his goodness, his beauty and love and holiness so that it covers us and draws us right into his heart. And there at the centre is Jesus himself, our great Good Shepherd, the One we've loved and now we see, who welcomes us and cares for us and leads us to springs of living water.

10. *Salvation is for living in a tough world.* Revelation 7 comes between Revelation 6 and Revelation 8 and 9. All three are fearsome chapters describing the stark realities of life in this world, a world where evil seems to be in charge and horrific things happen. Chapter 7 stands in stark contrast. Though God's people have to live in this evil world, and though we have to suffer as Jesus suffered, the book deliberately breaks from its description of our evil world to remind us of the tremendous fact of our salvation. Take the opportunity, then, to turn away from the harsh realities of the world around, and draw fresh strength from the deeper reality of your salvation. Stand with this white

robed multitude before the throne of God. Be refreshed by the vision of what God's got in store for you; for a time it may be 'great tribulation'; but one day it will be great joy. Sometimes you may wonder if you'll ever make it through. Be encouraged. God knows you and has put his seal upon you; he has promised to keep you. Maybe you feel all on your own, or that God's people are so small and weak compared with all the rest. Rejoice, God's kingdom is big; God's people are a multitude no-one can number. Drink deep at the rich truths of your salvation. Then you can get things in focus and face the world around you; then you can cope with Revelation 6, 8 and 9, with suffering and the awful ravages of sin and evil in our world. Then, too, you can get on with the great task of living out your great salvation on each of the days God calls you to stay here on planet earth.

Am I saved? Thank you, Lord, that I can be, and that I can be sure. Salvation belongs to you and you give it now to me as you give me Jesus the Saviour. I receive him; I welcome him as my Saviour, my Lord and my God. Live in me, Saviour God, and enable me to live out the wonder of your salvation.

20.

Abraham and the God who blesses

Someone once said the Old Testament begins with a curse and ends with a curse. That's a pretty sombre way of putting things, though it's true that within the first three or four pages God is having to pronounce a curse on the serpent for the way he has spoilt his beautiful creation. The final words of the final book in the Old Testament are a promise that a new Elijah would come to right what is wrong among God's people lest God comes and strikes the land 'with a curse' (Gen. 3:14; Mal. 4:6).

But cursing is not the name of the game with God. For him it is the opposite. Our God is the God who blesses. After eleven chapters of the mess that the devil and the human race have made of the world, Genesis 12 starts the story of God's purposes of grace and salvation. He sets out his plan to Abraham in no uncertain terms:

'I will make you into a great nation
    and I will bless you;
I will make your name great,
    and you will be a blessing.

I will bless those who bless you,
   and whoever curses you I will curse;
and all peoples on earth
   will be blessed through you.' (Gen. 12:2-3)

Five times in these two verses God speaks of blessing. His call to Abraham is a call to be blessed and to be a blessing and to be the means through which all the world would receive God's blessing. That call was passed on from Abraham to his descendants and comes to us today: God calls you and me to be blessed, to be a blessing, and to be the means through which the whole world is blessed.

Though it's a common word in the Bible, the word 'bless' is out of fashion these days, and many of us would be hard put to give it a clear definition. In the Bible the words 'bless' and 'blessed' are used both of God and of humans, and it may be helpful to start with their meaning when applied to God before understanding what they mean in a human context.

When Jesus was on trial before the Sanhedrin, the high priest asked him directly if he was the Christ, the Son of God. But since the name of God was too holy to be spoken, he used the phrase 'the Blessed One' instead (Mk. 14:61). Paul uses the same phrase a number of times, though the NIV translators change it to 'praised' (e.g. Rom. 9:5). When writing to Timothy he speaks of 'the glorious gospel of the blessed God' and 'God, the blessed and only Ruler, the King of kings and Lord of lords, who lives in unapproachable light' (1 Tim. 1:11, 6:15).

God is the blessed one; he lives in eternal blessedness. Some Bible versions translate 'blessed' as 'happy', but that seems much too weak a word to describe the blessedness of God, the depths of his joy, the richness of his peace, his perfect wholeness. In God is everything that is good: life, truth, holiness, beauty and so much more. All these things enrich his life and make up his profound and glorious blessedness.

But the amazing truth is that God doesn't keep the blessedness he enjoys to himself. He wants to share it with others. Not only is he blessed; he longs to bless. He wants others to share the riches of his joy, the fullness of his peace, the wonders of what he enjoys. That was what he meant when he announced his purposes of blessing to Abraham. That was what Paul was talking about when he wrote to the Ephesians, using the word 'bless' three times in one verse, 'Blessed be [NIV "Praise be to"] the God and Father of our Lord Jesus Christ, who has blessed us in the heavenly realms with every spiritual blessing in Christ' (Eph. 1:3). The blessedness God experiences in heaven has been poured out on us.

Back at the time of the Exodus God expressed his desire to bless his people in this way:

> The LORD said to Moses, 'Tell Aaron and his sons, "This is how you are to bless the Israelites. Say to them:
>
> > "The LORD bless you
> >   and keep you;
> > the LORD make his face shine upon you
> >   and be gracious to you;
> > the LORD turn his face towards you
> >   and give you peace."
>
> 'So they will put my name on the Israelites, and I will bless them.' (Num. 6:22-27)

There are several things we can learn about God's blessing from this passage.

- *He wants us to have it.* We don't have to try and squeeze blessings out of a mean and grudging God. Here God takes the initiative; he commands the priests to speak his blessing on the people. He's more ready to bless than we are to be blessed.

- *The heart of blessing is the Lord himself.* The words 'The LORD', repeated three times, are strongly emphasized. God isn't tossing us bits of blessing out of heaven, a parcel of peace here and a lump of love there; the blessing he gives is himself, and he is the LORD. He is the God who comes, and as he comes his blessing comes with him.

- *Blessing means keeping.* He's the God who watches over us, who cares and protects us. His strong arm and gentle hand are placed on our lives. Nehemiah was conscious of it when he used the phrase, 'the gracious hand of my God was upon me' (Neh. 2:9). Jesus put his hand upon the children as he blessed them; our God keeps his hand upon our lives.

- *Blessing means God's shining face.* Moses saw it on Sinai; John saw it on Patmos: the light and the glory and radiance of the face of the living God. 'For God who said, "Let light shine out of darkness," made his light shine in our hearts to give us the light of the knowledge of the glory of God in the face of Christ' (2 Cor. 4:6).

- *Blessing means grace.* This isn't us begging God to be gracious to us; this is God freely and generously pouring his grace out upon us.

- *Blessing means God's face turned towards us.* That's the opposite of God turning his face away and rejecting us. It's back to Jesus and the children, the welcoming smile, the open arms. It's the lost son's father, with the embrace and the kiss and the best robe and the ring. It's the open door, the throne of grace to which we can come with confidence.

- *Blessing is peace.* Peace in the Bible is much more than calm; it's healing and wholeness, becoming the people God made us to be, relationships restored, brokenness repaired, living in the light of his life and goodness. And it is a gift.

- *Blessing is the name of God upon us.* The priests in the Old Testament days put God's name on the people (Num. 6:27). It was the great name, the LORD, the I AM, the living, eternal, almighty God. We, too, have been baptized into the name of this mighty God, the Father, the Son and the Holy Spirit (Mt. 28:19). God takes up his pen and writes his name over our lives. All his resources, 'every spiritual blessing' are opened up to us. A cheque unsigned is worth nothing, even though it's made out for a £1,000,000. It's still worth nothing if it's signed by someone who hasn't a penny in the bank. But if a multimillionaire signs it, then it's worth a million. God puts his name on us, and, because he's a multimillionaire, we're worth a million!

God promised to bless Abraham. But he went further. He promised to make Abraham a blessing to others, and, ultimately, to bless the whole world through him. That's God's purpose for you and me as well, and for all his people. He sees a world that is hurting and struggling, that desperately needs his peace and joy and goodness. And he calls us to be the means through which his blessing reaches out to everyone in it.

For Abraham the call to be the means through which God's blessing reached out to the world meant setting out on a journey of obedience and faith, 'even though he did not know where he was going' (Heb. 11:8). It meant being 'like a stranger in a foreign country', and trusting God even in impossible situations (Heb. 11:9,11,17-19).

For us too it will mean a journey of obedience and faith, taking us to places and into situations we least expect, but constantly giving us opportunities of bringing God's blessing into the lives of others. It may be that God will choose to use our lives to bless thousands, as we preach to large crowds or give lots of money to feed those who are hungry.

Whether this happens or not he will certainly call us to be a blessing to others in a whole range of small ways. I have a shrewd suspicion that in his book the small things we do to bless others are just as significant as the big ones.

There's no shortage of 'small' ways we can be a blessing to others, but in case you can't think of any, here are a few suggestions.

- *Make the effort to scatter mini-blessings around.* Smile at the people you pass in the street. Tell the guy who's picking up the litter that he's doing a great job. Let someone else go in front of you in the queue. Affirm people; be an encourager; be quick to praise; say 'Thank you.'

- *Pray for people.* You don't need to let them know – although for many people knowing that you care enough to spend time praying for them will itself be

a blessing. Lift them up in your prayers and place
them and their situation in the hands of God. Ask
God to pour his peace and goodness and love into
their lives.

- *Be determined to take with you something of the presence
  of the Lord wherever you go.* We've all met people who
  manage to spread gloom and depression wherever
  they go; our calling is to be the opposite. 'God' wrote
  Paul, 'always leads us in triumphal procession in
  Christ and through us spreads everywhere the fra-
  grance of the knowledge of him' (2 Cor. 2:14). Even if
  you don't feel particularly 'triumphal', still make the
  effort; resist the pressure to moan or be miserable; let
  his light shine through you.

- *Spread the blessing of the gospel.* The best blessing we
  can pass on to anyone is, of course, Jesus himself.
  We can show them Jesus in our lives, and we can
  speak of him in our words. You can be pretty certain
  that among your neighbours or those you work
  with are many who do not know the gospel. Just as
  God chose Abraham and put him where he wanted
  him, he has chosen you and put you next to them.
  He has given you a message to pass on to them, and
  the anointing of the Holy Spirit to show you how
  and when to do it, and to make your witness effective.

How about a little exercise to end this chapter? Take a
piece of paper and list all the people you will meet this
coming week. Put an asterisk by anyone who seems in
special need of God's blessing. Then go through the list
working out how you can be a means of blessing to
them. When you come to those with an asterisk, think up

a double blessing for them, something really special. Then pray over the list – and put it into practice.

> *God of blessing, I welcome you. The Lord bless me, and keep me. The Lord make his face shine upon me and be gracious to me. The Lord turn his face towards me and give me peace. The Lord make me a blessing to others. The Lord bless his people and make each one a blessing so that through us all the peoples on earth will be blessed.*

21.

Frightened fishermen and the power of God

They were used to the sudden squalls that swept down on the Lake of Galilee from the surrounding hills. Though fierce, they were usually short lived, and Peter, Andrew, James and John had had plenty of experience coping with them. But this one was different. The wind was furious, the waves were the highest they had ever seen; the little boats didn't stand a chance; wave after wave was rolling over them; soon they would be full, and that would be the end. This time it wasn't just the landsmen who were terrified.

All the time Jesus was asleep in the stern. Anyone who could sleep through that storm must have been pretty tired. But he couldn't just be left there. So they woke him shouting these words that were both a rebuke and a cry for help: 'Teacher, don't you care if we drown?' The next moments were shattering, an experience of the God of power they would never forget. Jesus got up and spoke to the storm, words of authority and power: 'Quiet! Be still!' And the wind stopped, and the sea was completely calm.

Maybe the disciples had been expecting something when they shook Jesus awake. They had seen plenty of miracles, and they knew this man had the power to rescue them. But this was something different. This was power over the storm. He could speak a word and the screaming wind stopped dead. Another word and the raging waves disappeared. Those in the boat who were fishermen, and several of the others who lived by the lakeshore, were all too familiar with storms on the lake. They knew that winds don't stop dead in their tracks; waves too continue – often for hours after a storm. But here, at the words of Jesus the sea was like glass.

If they had been frightened before, they were even more frightened now. But it wasn't terror and panic in the face of imminent death. This time it was a heavy sense of fear and dread. What they had seen was awesome: power that could only be the power of the Creator God. 'Who is this?' they cried. 'Even the wind and the waves obey him' (Mk. 4:35-41).

The answer to their question, of course, was that this man was God. For a moment his almighty overwhelming power – power that flung stars into space and created the amazing energy that lies in every atom, was unveiled. Only for a moment. God incarnate chose to come to this world in weakness and gentleness, and he resisted the temptation to seek to win followers through acts of spectacular supernatural power. But what they saw in that moment was the real thing, the mighty power of their God.

A close encounter with the power of God isn't necessarily a pleasant experience. But you can be sure that those frightened fishermen came out of that encounter with something they would never lose: the knowledge that nothing was too hard for their God. If Jesus can silence the storm with a word, then anyone who has him in their lives has nothing to fear. At times, being human, they may have allowed their knowledge of this fact to be eclipsed by circumstances, as Peter did when confronted with a servant girl in the courtyard of the high priest. Even so, what they had experienced remained, and, coupled with the power of God demonstrated in the resurrection of Jesus, formed the basis for their beliefs and actions.

'We did not follow cleverly invented stories when we told you about the power and the coming of our Lord Jesus Christ, but we were eye-witnesses of his majesty,' wrote Peter, some thirty years later (2 Pet. 1:16). 'His divine power has given us everything we need for life and godliness through our knowledge of him who called us by his own glory and goodness' (2 Pet. 1:3).

The church of Jesus Christ today is weak – and that's a very good thing. The days when bishops and popes wielded secular power, and state churches used their position to further their ends are mercifully over. We are called to walk with Jesus the way of weakness; 'God chose the foolish [or weak] things of the world to shame the wise. He chose the lowly things of this world and the despised things – and the things that are not – to nullify the things that are, so that no-one may boast before him' (1 Cor. 1:27-29). 'We're just clay jars' says Paul, 'very ordinary, very fragile.'

But in the clay jars is a treasure. In the church of Jesus Christ is the living God. In our weakness is his almighty power. 'We have this treasure in jars of clay to show that this all-surpassing power is from God and not from us.' 'He said to me, "My grace is sufficient for you, for my power is made perfect in weakness"' (2 Cor. 4:7, 12:9). God may well call us to struggle and suffer. But we can be confident that his power is always there working through our weakness, and ready to spring into action any time it's needed.

Most of us don't have too much difficulty in accepting that God is in us. We've asked him into our lives; we believe he's come. The Father and the Son have made their home in us; God has poured his Holy Spirit into our hearts. But we find it harder to grasp and put into practice what this actually means. Jesus may be there, but he's way back at the stern of the boat, on the raised bit where the waves aren't breaking, nice and comfortable on a cushion, and he's fast asleep.

Meanwhile we're battling with the storm, struggling with our fears and doubts, about to be overwhelmed by the waves, faced with the prospect of the whole lot going under: us, the boat, and even Jesus himself. So what do we do? Battle forward on our own, because we think that we'll be able to make it without any help from Jesus? Go it alone because we don't actually believe that Jesus would be able to do anything: if we woke him up he would only get in the way? Or maybe we leave Jesus sleeping because we know that if he woke up and did something we might find it disturbing, even terrifying; better to leave him comfortable in the Jesus slot, and not let him loose on real life. So we battle on on our own, and all the time the God of power is sleeping at the back.

When Paul prayed for the Ephesians he included a prayer for power. But he didn't pray that God would make them powerful, or even that he would do powerful things among them. He prayed that they would know God's power. Of course, one way of knowing it would be to experience it as the frightened fishermen did; but another way is to grasp the truth of it, to get hold of its reality in our minds. I fancy that that is what Paul was praying for in his prayer for the Ephesians. It's a matter of grasping the magnitude of God's power by an act of faith, just as we grasp the Christian hope – the riches of what God has prepared for us – by an act of faith.

I keep asking that the God of our Lord Jesus Christ, the glorious Father, may give you the Spirit of wisdom and revelation, so that you may know him better. I pray also that the eyes of your heart may be enlightened in order that you may know the hope to which he has called you, the riches of his glorious inheritance in the saints, and his incomparably great power for us who believe. That power is like the working of his mighty strength, which he exerted in Christ when he raised him from the dead and seated him at his right hand in the heavenly realms, far above all rule and authority, power and dominion. (Eph. 1:17-21)

So here's a challenge; to get hold of what it really means to have a God of power living in us. To wrap our minds round the implications of Christ stilling the storm, or raising the dead, or dismissing demons with a word. To get our hearts fired up with the reality of the resurrection, and the knowledge that our Saviour is now on the throne of the universe, far above all other powers, with 'all things under his feet' (Eph. 1:22). If we could really get hold of these things, what a difference it would make to our faith and lives. With such a powerful God in us we need fear nothing; persecution, suffering, setbacks, pressures, demonic opposition, problems, the future – nothing is greater than the power of our God in us.

Writing about 'false prophets' and 'the spirit of the antichrist' John wrote, 'You, dear children, are from God and have overcome them, because the one who is in you is greater than the one that is in the world' (1 Jn. 4:4). Listing just about every problem and opposition that Christians may meet, Paul declared, 'What, then, shall we say in response to this? If God is for us, who can be against us?... In all these things we are more than conquerors through him who loved us' (Rom. 8:31,37).

So here's the challenge; to move from merely holding the theological doctrine that God is powerful to being gripped and energized by the awareness that this great God of power is in you and will never fail you. He will work out his amazing purposes even through your weakness. To help do this you may like to commit the following verses to memory, and bring them out when you find you're beginning to forget who it is who lives in you.

The kingdom of God is not a matter of talk but of power. (1 Cor. 4:20)

The weapons we fight with are not the weapons of the world. On the contrary, they have divine power to demolish strongholds. (2 Cor. 10:4)

[He] is able to do immeasurably more than all we ask or imagine, according to his power that is at work within us. (Eph. 3:20)

Be strong in the Lord and in his mighty power. (Eph. 6:10)

I want to know Christ and the power of his resurrection. (Phil. 3:10)

I can do everything through him who gives me strength. (Phil. 4:13)

God has said,
    'Never will I leave you;
    never will I forsake you.'
So we say with confidence,
    'The Lord is my helper; I will not be afraid.
    What can man do to me?' (Heb. 13:5-6)

God of power, Lord God Almighty, teach me what it means to have you living in me. Help me to ignore those voices that say you're powerless or a million miles away. Remind me of your nearness and your power in those times when I'm weak and the powers of evil seem so strong. From now on may your power be a continuing reality in my life.

22.

Corinth and the wisdom and foolishness of God

Acts 18:1-11, 1 Corinthians 1:18-2:16

Corinth Courier, 3rd June AD 50.

Yet another new religion is trying to get a foothold in Corinth. Paul (alias Saul) of Tarsus arrived in the city last week and has already started propagating his new brand of Judaism. At present he's resident in the tentmakers' area of the city, and last Saturday he preached in the Jewish synagogue. His sermon provoked heated discussion, though as yet there are no reports of riots like those he has said to have caused recently in Thessalonica and Berea.

Crispus, the ruler of the synagogue, told our reporter that Paul is claiming that his new religion is the logical fulfilment of the Jewish religion, which had promised the coming of a saviour who would sort out the mess the world is in. He claims that this saviour has come but that he was executed in Jerusalem some seventeen years ago. Paul appears to be making two new claims about this person: that he was in fact a god, or rather God, since Jews think there's only one God, and that after he was dead he came back to life. It hardly seems likely that such far-fetched ideas will be accepted by many, though the new religion has apparently won some followers during Paul's recent visit to Athens.

Corinth Courier, 4th June AD 50.

Dear Sir,

Your splendid paper carried a brief report yesterday of the arrival in our great city of Paul (alias Saul) of Tarsus. Though you mentioned in passing that this man has caused trouble at Thessalonica and Berea, the tone of your report was dangerously neutral. Our cosmopolitan city already contains a huge variety of religious superstitions; in the normal course of events one extra wouldn't matter much, but Paul's religion is particularly dangerous and its propagation should be resisted vehemently.

I have reliable reports from colleagues in the Athenian Philosophical Association of what Paul taught while he was in Athens. From start to finish, his religion is nonsense. It is illogical, irrational, total foolishness. If, as Paul claims, a god came to live on earth it is inconceivable that he would live the kind of life that Jesus, Paul's God, is supposed to have lived. No god would allow himself to be born in poverty, brought up in obscurity, spend a few years in Galilee and Judea of all places, and then let himself be executed. One doesn't need to be a philosopher to realize that all this is ridiculous; anyone with a modicum of wisdom can see that it could not possibly be true.

I forbear to mention the myth of resurrection from the dead, something modern science has shown to be impossible.

I trust that none of the readers of your excellent paper will be carried away by this dangerous nonsense.

Yours faithfully,
Archilogos,
Chair, Corinthian Philosophical Association

Corinth Courier, 18th June AD 50.

Dear Sir,

May I respond to a recent letter from Archilogos, chair of the Corinthian Philosophical Association, about the religion currently being preached in Corinth by Paul.

I am a follower of this religion and a colleague of Paul and have recently arrived from Berea, where a good number of citizens have become believers.

Archilogos states that no-one with a 'modicum of wisdom' could possibly believe in this religion. He is wrong. By no stretch of the imagination can the believers at Berea be called foolish or superstitious. Many of them are intelligent and hard-headed Jews (I'm a Jew myself, and know how hard-headed we can be). There are also many Greek men, some of whom are members of the Berean Philosophical Association. What is more, there are a number of prominent Greek women, capable and intelligent people who would never swallow something 'irrational' or 'ridiculous'.

There's no space in this letter to defend all the truths about Jesus; any of your readers who wish to check them are most welcome to hear Paul for themselves in the Jewish synagogue. But I will give a brief answer to the specific point Archilogos mentions.

He says that if God lived on earth he would not be born in poverty, live in obscurity, and so on. I agree, if this God is like most people's gods (and like most people who invent them) – out to feather his own nest, only interested in looking after himself. But suppose God actually loves the world he has made, and really cares for those who are poor and hurting and weak. Surely there's nothing crazy about such a God getting alongside the poor and weak? Suppose, too, that he so loves the world that he chooses to break the power of evil and death which holds us all in its grip; and suppose the only way to do this is to experience evil and death and so break its power – and then show that he's done that by rising from the dead. We might think that such love is amazing, almost incredible, but it's certainly not foolish. In my book it's staggeringly brilliant, the best news the world has ever heard, more wonderful than all the discoveries of the wise.

Yours faithfully,
Silas

Corinth Courier, 25th June AD 50.

Dear Sir,

May I add my comments to those recently published in your columns by Archilogos and Silas.

As ruler of the Corinth synagogue where Paul has been based these past few weeks I've had plenty of opportunity to examine this new religion which Archilogos calls 'foolishness' and 'ridiculous'. Your readers may be interested in my conclusions.

1. There's nothing foolish about Paul. He's as hardheaded as any of us Jews; what's more he has a brilliant logical mind that Plato would have been proud of. But, though I don't doubt he would be capable of them, he refuses to use rhetorical tricks or clever arguments to persuade people. He states his case clearly and simply, and, as he would say, leaves it to God to convince his hearers of its truth.

2. Paul himself started out as a keen critic and opponent of Jesus. What changed him was a dynamic experience of meeting this Jesus some time after he had been executed. This, as your readers can imagine, was mind-blowing, but Paul set himself to work through all its implications, and found that not only does the resurrection of Jesus fit perfectly with the Jewish religion in which he had been brought up; the whole thing in fact makes perfect sense. If Jesus is God, then of course he's more powerful than death. If God does care for people, then it's not surprising he shows himself to them.

3. The weak point in Paul's case, in my opinion, is that God died on a cross. Paul argues convincingly that this was in fact prophesied in our Jewish Scriptures, but many of us Jews find it a major stumbling block. But, unlike Archilogos, we're willing to keep an open mind; maybe if God were to give us one or two miraculous signs, as he gave to Paul, then we too would become believers.

Yours faithfully,
Crispus,
Ruler, Corinth Synagogue

Corinth Courier, 7th August AD 50.

The new Jewish sect that has recently spread to Corinth has seen two significant developments in the last few days. According to reports there has been a showdown between Paul, the prophet of the new movement, and some of the many Jews who attend the synagogue in our city. Paul has been using the synagogue as his base for several weeks, and has been arguing that the one true God came to earth to show us his love and truth and that he lived among the Jews for some thirty years until he was executed under Pontius Pilate. But, being God, he rose from death, thus vindicating all his claims and teaching, and is available to live in anyone who is willing to trust and receive him.

Though some have accepted this new teaching, some have been unhappy about it, feeling it undermines what they have traditionally held. As a result they made a strong attack on Paul a few days ago; he has now severed his connections with the synagogue, and started holding meetings in the adjacent house of Titius Justus. We understand that a good number of the synagogue members – including Crispus, the ruler of the synagogue, and his household – have joined him there, and that many Corinthian citizens are being baptized into the new movement.

Corinth Courier, 12th August AD 50.

Dear Sir,

I am appalled to learn from your splendid paper that Crispus, the ruler of the Jewish synagogue – until recently a respected member of our multi-racial Corinthian community – has so far departed from the ways of wisdom and sanity as to become a follower of this new religion that worships Jesus as God. It is hard to conceive how any intelligent person can accept the nonsense that there is but one God, that he actually loves human beings and that he came to live on earth in obscurity and poverty. It is even more impossible to believe that he suffered and died as a criminal, that he rose again, that he is able to live in those who believe in him, and that one day he'll be the judge of the whole world. Could anything be more far-fetched? I am profoundly sad that anyone who claims to have any intelligence at all should be prepared to embrace it.

I have one comfort, however. Anything as preposterous as this new religion won't last. I give it ten years. Mark my words; by then reason and wisdom will have prevailed, people like Crispus will see the error of their ways, and this teaching will be no more.

Yours in anticipation,
Archilogos,
Chair, Corinthian Philosophical Association

Corinth Courier, 1st September AD 50.

Dear Sir,

Some of my friends have urged me to write stating my own position on some of the issues that have been raised in the *Corinth Courier* in the past few weeks regarding the gospel that I preach concerning Jesus Christ, the Son of God.

I can understand the vehemence with which Archilogos attacks my gospel. I was vehemently opposed to it once, as well. But then, God in his grace met me and called me to preach a gospel I had once ridiculed. May the same happen to Archilogos.

Yes, to the scholar and the philosopher of this age, the gospel is foolishness. But then, to God much of the wisdom of the world is foolishness. Is it not foolish for men, even wise men, to assume that they can understand God and all his ways with their little minds? Isn't God infinitely greater than the wisest of us, and his purposes far beyond our understanding? Is not the wise man the one who realizes the limits of his understanding? Didn't Socrates himself say that the only knowledge he has is that he knows nothing? Yes, my gospel says that God came to earth to live in obscurity and weakness, something the wise find hard to comprehend. But the foolishness of God is wiser than man's wisdom, and the weakness of God is stronger than man's strength.

I grant that, with some notable exceptions, most of those who have become believers in Jesus here in Corinth are ordinary people. Not many members of the Corinthian Philosophical Association and not many of noble birth have followed the Way. Perhaps that's because cleverness and status and wealth are always a barrier between us and the true God. Jesus taught that we have to lay aside all our human achievements and become like little children to enter his kingdom. In his wisdom he's chosen the foolish and the weak to shame the wise and the strong.

May I through your columns make a suggestion to Archilogos and any others of your readers who find it hard to make sense of the life and teaching of Jesus? Ask God to show you the truth through his Holy Spirit, that he may open your mind to things as they really are, not to what our limited understanding makes them. Without the Spirit no-one will ever be able to grasp God's truth; but through the Spirit what would otherwise be foolishness becomes the wisdom of God.

Perhaps Archilogos is well-experienced in praying. In case he isn't, may I suggest the following prayer?

Living God, Creator of all, wise beyond the greatest of philosophers, whose ways are good and wonderful, greater than anything we could conceive, have mercy on me in my ignorance and foolishness. Like Socrates I seek the truth and am willing to follow wherever the truth may lead, even if that means I will have to let go of my most cherished beliefs. Lord, by your Spirit show me the truth; what's more, enable me to receive the truth and for the rest of my life to follow the truth. Amen.

Grace and peace to you,
Paul

*Thank you Lord for giving me a brain; thank you
for wisdom and discernment. But I don't want my
cleverness ever to become a barrier between me
and you. I accept that your wisdom, even those
bits that seem to me foolishness, is so much wiser
than mine. So I give you my brain, my mind, my
thinking. Lord of all, be Lord there too; teach me
your truth; lead me in your wisdom.*

23.

The lost son and the grace of God

'If you want to see the grace of God,' says John, 'look at Jesus. See him touching the leper. See him talking with the woman at the well. See him welcoming the children. See him with the woman taken in adultery. Stand before his cross and hear him praying for his enemies. We have seen his glory, full of grace.'

'If you want to see the grace of God,' says Peter, 'look at me. I blew it. Absolutely. Totally. Finally. In his moment of need I cursed and swore that I never knew him. In that moment I smashed my relationship with him; I turned my back on all that he had meant to me through those three great years. I nailed him to the cross. I finished everything. And he picked me up. "Go and tell my disciples... and Peter," he said. He came to me. He didn't even tell me off. He reached out to me. And he forgave me. And trusted me to serve him. I tell you, that is grace – amazing grace.'

'If you want to see the grace of God,' says Paul, 'look at me. I fought him. I hated him. I cursed his name. I persecuted him and his followers. I laughed when they stoned Stephen. I was determined to stamp him out for ever. And then he came to me. And forgave me. And called me. And made me his. Overflowing, overwhelming grace. And all the way through, when things were tough, when I wasn't sure if I could keep going, he said, "My grace is sufficient for you." That's grace, abundant grace, poured out on me.'

'If you want to see the grace of God,' says Jesus, 'listen to the story of the lost son. See that waiting father, day by day, week by week, year by year watching the long road in case his boy should return. Watch the son trudging hopelessly back, his life ruined, his sonship forfeited, his soul polluted with sin and evil. "No longer worthy to be called your son." But desperate, desperate for food. "Treat me like a slave – but give me something to eat!" But when he was still a long way away, his father saw him, and his heart went out to him, and he ran to his son, and he threw his arms around his neck, and he kissed him, and he welcomed him, and he forgave him. He called to the servants, "Quick, bring the best robe, not any old robe, but the best one. Put a ring on his finger and sandals on his feet – no way will I treat him like a slave. And get some food – the best food. Make it a feast. Make it a celebration. Because this is my son, dead but now alive, lost but now found."'

That's a good story. Now let me tell you three shocking ones. The first is about an employer who took on daily casual workers. Before they started they agreed to the standard hourly rate. Half way through the day he took on some more workers. Just before closing time he took on some more. At the end of the day he handed out the pay packets. Everyone got the same. Those who had worked all day got what they expected – a day's pay for a day's work. But those who'd only worked half a day or an hour or so got the same. Of course, the all-day workers were furious. But the man stuck to his guns. 'Don't I have the right to do what I want with my own money? Or are you envious because I am generous?' (Mt. 20:15).

The second shocking story is a sequel to the lost son (Lk. 15:11-24). It's the big brother moaning. 'It's not right. It's not fair. Here am I, the good guy, working hard all the time, doing the work of two to make up for that brother of mine who's spent all the family savings on prostitutes. You never threw a party for me, never even let me have a goat so I could have a party with my friends. Yet when he comes, filthy and polluted, you welcome him back with open arms and kill the fattened calf. Where's the justice in that? Never mind him; where's your love for me, the good guy?' 'My son,' said the father, 'you are always with me, and all I have is yours. But there's no way I'm not going to make a fuss over my son who was dead and now is alive, who was lost and now is found' (Lk. 15:25-32).

Story number three is right up to date. It concerns two churches. One of them is in a remote area of a South American country. It's a Pentecostal church, belonging to a local grouping that has some pretty weird ideas and practices. There's no pastor, and almost all the members are poor and poorly educated. The large majority of them are very immature Christians. None of them have ever received any decent Bible teaching, and their Christian beliefs are all mixed up with ideas left over from their pre-Christian days. Their lives, too, though showing some evidence of the work of the Spirit, still contain many things that are decidedly not Christian.

The other church is in a prosperous city suburb in the UK. It's full of well-educated, mature, sound evangelical Christians. It gets the best of Bible teaching from its large staff of theologically trained ministers. Its theology and

practice are faultless. Though there are some evidences of
the presence of God in the UK church, if you want to see
God clearly present and obviously at work you would
need to go to the South American church. Despite its
unorthodoxy and immaturity, that's where you'll find a
steady stream of conversions, spectacular healings, genuine miracles and the manifest presence of the living God.

Here are eight truths concerning the grace of God that
are illustrated by Jesus' story of the lost son.

1. *The background to grace is sin.* The picture Jesus paints of
    how God sees us is pretty sobering. It's not a matter of
    having a few problems or making a few mistakes. Like
    the son, we've deliberately turned our back on our
    Father, spurning his love, rejecting his fatherhood, and
    refusing to serve and obey him. Then we've wasted
    what he's given us, using our 'inheritance', such as our
    lives, our bodies, our time, our skills, and the earth's
    resources to satisfy our own selfish desires. And finally,
    we've ended up with the pigs, a graphic element of the
    story that to Jesus' Jewish hearers would have indica-
    ted that we're totally polluted and as far from God as
    we possibly could be. This may hardly be how we see
    ourselves, but it's how God sees us.

2. *In grace God makes the first move.* It wasn't that the
    father happened to glance out of the window on the
    day his son returned and so just chanced to see him.
    The picture Jesus paints is of a father who kept going
    out to look for his boy, just as the shepherd went out
    to look for the lost sheep. 'While we were still sinners,
    Christ died for us' (Rom. 5:8). While the son was still
    squandering his money in the distant country, with
    no thought of ever returning home, his father was
    watching and preparing to welcome him back.

3. *Grace is unearned and undeserved.* Jesus makes this quite clear in the case of the lost son. He'd deliberately renounced his sonship; he'd spent all his inheritance; he'd dragged the family name in the mud. He deserved nothing from his father. Rightly he said, 'I am no longer worthy to be called your son' (Lk. 15:21). At best he could offer to be a servant, and even then his father was under no obligation to employ him.

4. *Grace isn't fussy.* What was it that drove the son to start the long journey home? It wasn't awareness of his sin or a deep longing to restore his broken relationship with his father. It was hunger. Another self-centred physical desire, not a thousand miles removed from the desires he'd been so busy gratifying for the last few years. The goal of the journey home was food, not father. True, his desperate hunger helped him see the error of his ways and forced a confession of sin from him, but I'm not sure he'd ever have confessed his sin if his money hadn't run out. But his father wasn't fussy. God's grace doesn't wait until we've got all our motives sorted out. He doesn't check that we're doctrinally sound before he blesses us.

5. *God's grace is God.* What, we might ask, does the son need? Food, for a start. And a bath and some decent clothes. Then we need to sit down and sort out his status and his role now he's back on the farm. What does he get? First and foremost, says Jesus, he gets his father. Make no mistake. God in his grace may give us gifts – strength, healing, wisdom, answers to prayer and so on. But grace is primarily and essentially God himself. Even food, the thing the boy would have felt

his greatest need, had to wait. What a picture; what a crazy undignified picture: the older man, throwing propriety to the winds, running along the rough track, his arms outstretched to embrace this filthy vagabond, to hold him, to kiss him, to draw him to himself. Later came the ring and the robe and the feast. But first it was the father. God's grace is God himself, the most amazing gift of all.

6. *God's grace is lavish.* Not any robe, but the best robe. Not just food, but a fattened calf feast. Not just a servant, but a son. That's our God. That's his grace.

7. *The tendency to question God's grace must be resisted.* We all have a sneaking sympathy for the elder brother. From his angle things weren't fair; he'd never even been allowed a goat party. The all-day workers, we feel, had some grounds for their grumbling: if the employer was in effect paying the late workers ten times the normal rate, why doesn't he pay the all-day team ten times the rate too? Why should God pour out such blessing on the South American church compared with the UK one? But, whatever our feelings may be, the Bible makes it clear that our grumbling and questioning and pushing God into a logical corner are wrong. The very essence of God's grace is that it is free, totally undeserved. God doesn't have to justify his generosity to us. If we could see the whole picture, of course, we would realize there's nothing to grumble about or question; it's only because our outlook is narrow and often tinged with selfishness that we find God's grace to others difficult. 'You are always with me, and everything I have is yours,' said the father to the elder son (Lk. 15:31). That glorious moment the younger son enjoyed, the embrace, the

robe and the ring – all this had been poured out on the elder son for years, if only he had been aware of it.

8. *God's grace is for celebrating and enjoying.* Forget the grumbling and the questioning. Give up trying to fit God's grace into your limited grid. It's there; it's big; all you have to do is accept it. If you're the younger son, let him embrace you and love you and clothe you in the best robe. Take the place of honour at the feast he spreads before you. Enjoy it, and love him for his grace. If you're the older brother, if you see God pouring out his grace into the lives of others, then rejoice. Be glad for them; be glad for God who finds such joy in being so generous and good. Be glad for yourself, for this gracious God is your God, and though you may not be directly aware of it, the same grace he's showing to others reaches out to you.

> *Hallelujah! That's my God! The God of grace, overflowing grace, amazing grace. I praise you; I'm so thrilled at the grace you've shown to me and to so many others. Go on, Lord; pour out more and more of your grace on our lives and our world, for the glory of your name and the coming of your kingdom.*

24.

Jacob and the God of hurt and healing

The playing field isn't level. 'We are not born equal.' Some are born in the UK; some in Somalia. Some are born healthy; some with a disability. Some have an easy life; for others it is tough. God rescued Peter from prison; he let Stephen be martyred. Paul prayed for others and they were healed; he asked God to take away the thorn in his flesh and God said 'No.'

Jacob started life in a malfunctioning family. His father, Isaac, loved his twin brother, Esau. His mother, Rebekah, loved Jacob. He was born clutching Esau's heel, so they gave him the name 'Heel', a word which in Hebrew also means 'Supplanter' or 'Trickster'. That set the agenda for the first part of his life, tricking his brother out of his birthright, and tricking his father into giving him his blessing. Esau swore to kill him in revenge, so Jacob fled to his uncle, Laban. There he was on the receiving end of trickery, at the hands of Laban, though in the end he gave as good as he got (Gen. 25:21-34, 27:1-31:55).

During the twenty years he stayed with Laban, Jacob lived in fear of Esau. We pick up his story as he is returning with wives and children and flocks, knowing that Esau is coming to meet him, complete with 400 men. In fear Jacob divides his company in two, cries out to God for help, arranges for groups of servants to drive herds ahead of him as gifts for Esau in an attempt to buy off his anger, and sends his immediate family and 'all his possessions' on ahead.

> Jacob was left alone, and a man wrestled with him till daybreak. When the man saw that he could not overpower him, he touched the socket of Jacob's hip so that his hip was wrenched as he wrestled with the man. Then the man said, 'Let me go, for it is daybreak.'
>
> But Jacob replied, 'I will not let you go unless you bless me.'
>
> The man asked him, 'What is your name?'
>
> 'Jacob,' he answered.
>
> Then the man said, 'Your name will no longer be Jacob, but Israel, because you have struggled with God and with men and have overcome.'
>
> Jacob said, 'Please tell me your name.'
>
> But he replied, 'Why do you ask my name?' Then he blessed him there.
>
> So Jacob called the place Peniel, saying, 'It is because I saw God face to face, and yet my life was spared.'
>
> The sun rose above him as he passed Peniel, and he was limping because of his hip. (Gen. 32:24-31)

Perhaps when the man started wrestling with him, Jacob thought that he represented Esau, the brother whom he'd tricked, and whom he feared. But by the time he had finished he knew the man was much more than that: 'I saw God face to face.'

All night they wrestled. All his life had been a struggle, a wrestling with circumstances, with others, with

God. And neither side won. Jacob was neither defeated by his life's experiences, nor did he triumph over them. He couldn't get on top of God, nor, as yet, had God got on top of him.

Then the man touched his hip socket. He deliberately injured him. Not to win the fight, for the next thing he does is ask Jacob to let him go. Rather, he injured him so that he would be damaged for life; from that day onward he walked with a limp.

*   *   *

Jacob, that's a nasty limp you've got. How long have you had it? How did you get it? Do you get a lot of pain with it?

Oh, I've had it for years, ever since I came back from Laban's place. Yes, it does hurt – it often keeps me awake at night. God gave me it.

You mean God deliberately hurt you?

Yes. He hurt me in lots of ways. He gave me a bad start in life; I couldn't relate to my dad, and my mother smothered me and controlled me. He gave me a twin brother who had everything, while I had nothing: a great physique, manly skills, and my father's love. And the biggest thing he had was the fact that he was the eldest son. They tell us we jostled each other in the womb. I can believe it. He pushed me out of the way so he could be born first and get all the privileges while I was con-demned to be 'the younger son', the number two, the one that didn't really matter. And they gave me that name 'Heel', laughing at me, just to rub it all in. They mocked me because I couldn't do the things Esau was so good at. When he and the men went out hunting I'd stay behind with the women, hiding away in the tents, trying to escape my dad's scorn because I was useless.

You say God was responsible for all the hurt you had to go through?

Yes, I think so. Not directly, perhaps, but ultimately. He could have sorted out my parents. He could have made sure I was born first. He could have given me an easy life. But he didn't. And I'm glad he didn't.

Why's that?

Well, it goes back to that night I wrestled with God. I'd always struggled with God, why he'd been so unfair towards me, what he was doing in my life, how he was going to keep his promises that he'd bless me and bless the whole world through me and my descendants. And that night I was desperate; for all I knew, within a few hours, Esau would have killed me and every one of my family. So I said, 'I will not let you go unless you bless me.'

And did he?

Yes, but not straightaway. First of all he gave me a new name. 'You're not going to be called "Heel" and "Trickster" any more. From now on you're a different man. Your name is "The one who struggles with God and overcomes."' I was shattered. It was so beautiful. All those struggles, all those hurts, all those dark years – struggling with God and overcoming! If I'd not had the hurts, I'd not have struggled. And if I hadn't struggled I wouldn't have overcome. And God wouldn't have given me my new name.

But what's in a name?

Quite a lot, at least in my culture. Your name describes you; it shapes your life. It's like someone who's being told all the time 'You're useless.' Tell your son that enough times, and he'll grow up convinced it's true. Tell your son he's a 'Heel' and he'll be one. But the real point with Israel, my new name, was that it was given me by God. If God says it, it's got to be. It was fantastic.

And then he blessed you?

I guess he'd already done so by giving me my new name and healing all the hurt of those dark years. At that moment I'm not sure I needed any more blessing. I felt so great, so lifted up, so near to God, I did something I'd never have dared to do: I asked him his name.

And did he tell you?

No. And rightly so. You see, in my culture having the name of God means having a handle on him, having control over him. It was really a bit of the old Jacob, still trying to manipulate, still trying to sort God out. And he drew the line at that. He remained mysterious, inscrutable, truly God. And that was right. It wasn't for me to try and understand him, to tell him what to do and how to handle my life. And after that night I didn't really need to. I could leave all that to him. But he did bless me.

So you came away with a damaged hip, a new name, and the blessing of God?

They were all the blessing of God. The damaged hip was a blessing; I could never take a step without remembering

how I got it. You won't believe how many times I've
thanked God for it.

*   *   *

Let's go forward nearly two thousand years to another man
who knew what it was to be hurt by God (see 2 Cor. 12:7-10).

*Paul, I've just been talking to Jacob, or 'Israel', as God named
him, about the time when he had that experience of wrestling
with God and God damaged his hip. For the rest of his life he
was crippled and suffered, yet he seemed glad about it. It was
a symbol of all the hurt God had allowed in his life, his struggle with it, and how he overcame and found healing when God
met him. It occurs to me your story's a bit the same.*

Well, everyone's story is different. God never deals with
two people in the same way. But, yes, I guess it's true that
God allowed all sorts of painful things to happen to me.
Some of them were easier to take than others. In a strange
way the floggings and the stonings didn't hurt me as
much as the times when my Christian friends let me
down, or when false teachers seemed to be undoing all
the work I'd done in the new churches. But I admit that
sometimes when I was in prison I really struggled with
what God was up to. I had such a vision for preaching the
gospel, and the need was so great, and there I was, week
after week, month after month, stuck in a stinking cell,
slowly rotting away. I tell you, there were times when I
was so frustrated and depressed I almost gave up.

Do you agree with Jacob that God deliberately made you suffer?

Putting it like that makes it sound as though God's being
cruel, or punishing me because I've done something

wrong. And of course neither of those is true. But, yes, I'm sure God called me to walk a hard road. He could have given me an easy life, but he didn't. But then, he could have made me good looking, but you can see for yourself he didn't!

I believe you had one particular experience that was a bit like Jacob and his hip.

You're thinking of my thorn, are you? As I said, God deals with everyone differently, but that's certainly something God's given me that hurts, and I've come to thank him for it.

Can you give us some more details?

Not about the thorn itself, except that it really hurts and the devil still has a great time exploiting it. But I'll tell you what God told me about it. I'd really prayed that he'd heal me. I didn't pray in a general way, but I set aside a day of prayer, and I got others to pray with me. But nothing happened. So we had another day of prayer. And still nothing happened. I might have given up then, but it was so bad I decided to try once more. We prayed fervently that last time, enough to melt the heart of the hardest God. And then he answered. Not by taking away the thorn, but by saying 'No'. And then he said something that was fantastic, something that didn't just make sense of the thorn, but made sense of all the other hurts he'd allowed into my life through the years. He said, 'My grace is sufficient for you, for my power is made perfect in weakness.' It was beautiful. It put everything into perspective.

So, despite your prayer, you never got healed?

I've still got the thorn; that's never been healed. But the hurt has been healed, not just the hurt of the thorn, but the hurt of all the other things that God allowed happen.

So from then on everything's been great?

You should be so lucky! If anything, life's got tougher. And of course I still get my down times, and I still struggle. But then I think back to what he said, and I remember that anything he allows into my life, even if it hurts, is ultimately for good, and that makes all the difference. I tell you honestly, that I have found I can actually delight in weaknesses and insults and hardships and persecutions and difficulties. When things are really tough, and I'm at my weakest, that's when God is at his greatest.

So you can thank God for giving you a thorn in your flesh?

I do, and for the beautiful thing he's done in me through it.

> **Lord, you know my hurt. You know how I feel about it, how I struggle. You know how I've cried out to you to take it away, and yet it's still there. You know the tears, the anger, the pain, the hopelessness. Lord, it's too much for me, too heavy to carry on my own. Help me. Do for me what you did for Jacob and Paul. Take my hurt, lift it up in your nail-pierced hands, and in your glorious grace and unfathomable wisdom turn it into a blessing.**

25.

Elijah and the God who refreshes

It's a strange story. Elijah has reached the pinnacle of his career. He's challenged Ahab, the evil king of Israel, to a showdown. Elijah and the God of Israel versus the 450 prophets of Baal and the gods that Jezebel, Ahab's wife, had introduced into the land. It took place on Mount Carmel in front of the king and his people, and it resulted in a stunning victory for Elijah and his God. In answer to Elijah's prayer that the Lord would demonstrate that he is the true God, the fire of God fell, and the people threw themselves on the ground, crying 'The LORD – he is God! The LORD – he is God!' (1 Kgs. 18:39)

And that wasn't all. For three years there had been a drought, and the people were facing disaster through famine. So Elijah went to the top of Carmel and prayed. Seven times he prayed, and at the seventh time a tiny cloud appeared in the sky. 'Go and tell Ahab,' said Elijah to his servant, '"Hitch up your chariot and go down before the rain stops you."' And rain it did, heavy rain, and lots of it. The drought was over; Elijah had saved the nation (1 Kgs. 18:19-46).

And then he ran away. At the moment of his greatest triumphs, when the whole nation was at his feet, he ran off into the desert because Jezebel had threatened to kill him. Not only did he run, but he gave up. 'He came to a broom tree, sat down under it and prayed that he might die. "I have had enough, LORD," he said. "Take my life; I am no better than my ancestors"' (1 Kgs. 19:4).

What's gone wrong? What's happened to the fearless prophet who confronted the king? Where's the man with such strength of faith and power in prayer? What about that amazing victory over the prophets of Baal? Can't the God who answers by fire and who brings water to the thirsty land take care of his prophet? All of it seems to have been forgotten, as Elijah gave up and asked to die.

The Bible story doesn't really tell us what had gone wrong. It's like Paul's thorn in the flesh; he doesn't give us the details – maybe because we all have different 'thorns' and it's easier for us to relate to what Paul is saying if we can imagine that our thorn might have been much the same as his. So here are a few suggestions of what might have gone wrong with Elijah; it could be that one or two will particularly resonate with you and your own situation.

- *A demonic counter-attack.* The powers of evil that lay behind the false gods weren't going to lie down and take defeat easily. There wasn't much they could do to rescue their prophets, but they could have a really good go at Elijah.

- *Physical exhaustion.* Quite apart from all his other exertions, Elijah finished the day on Mount Carmel by running in front of Ahab's chariot to Jezreel, a distance of some twenty-five miles. No wonder the man was exhausted.

- *Spiritual exhaustion.* When the woman in the crowd touched Jesus' robe and was healed, Jesus knew it because power had gone out from him (Lk. 8:46). Every spiritual battle we win or service we perform uses up something of our spiritual resources. Elijah was having a huge dose of preacher's Monday morning blues; he was spiritually drained.

- *Stress.* Elijah had lived with stress for years, as a lone voice in an enemy culture. It all climaxed in the events on Mount Carmel, and it left him shattered. Every stressful experience takes its toll; major traumatic experiences, like Carmel, can have serious and unexpected repercussions. Perhaps that's what was happening to Elijah.

- *Doubts.* We all struggle with doubts; some have a particular problem with self-doubt. It could be that Elijah's boldness before others masked his own inner struggles. Outwardly trusting, but inwardly struggling to cope. Outwardly confident, but inwardly unsure of himself.

- *Depression.* Some forms of depression show themselves by a swing from a high to a low. Elijah had been very high; now he was very low.

Maybe you could add other factors to the list, perhaps from your own experience. But it's time to turn to God's answer to Elijah, to the God who lifted him up and set him back on his feet – the God who refreshes.

It's interesting to find that God didn't sort Elijah out all at once. He did it in stages; in fact the process took the best part of six weeks. Sometimes it takes a lot longer. Yesterday someone came to see me who had been the pastor of a church he built up from 20 to 200 while coping with a very responsible full-time job in medical research. For five years afterwards he has suffered from depression. God's timetable is always a mystery to us; we want refreshing and healing and everything else at once. He's rarely in such a rush.

But the vital thing is that there in the desert, exhausted, disillusioned, and in despair, God came to Elijah. He was not alone. God was with him, every bit as much as he had been on Mount Carmel. Our problem is that we find it so much harder to trust that he's with us when we're down. In theory we know that our circumstances and feelings don't make the tiniest bit of difference to the reality of God's presence; but we all tend to be easy victims of our circumstances and feelings. Whatever Elijah may have felt, God through his angel was there in the desert with him (1 Kgs. 19:5).

The first stage in God's refreshing of Elijah contained two simple elements: food and sleep (1 Kgs. 19:5-7). I like that. It reminds me that God doesn't always have to solve our problems in some spectacular supernatural way. If we're weary or spiritually drained or struggling with pressure and stress, he tells us to use the resources he's already given us. If the problem is that we're doing too much, he tells us to shed some of the load. If we're being unfair to our body and not getting enough sleep or enough exercise, he tells us to sort ourselves out. If we're ignoring his Sabbath principle, he tells us to take time out or to have a sabbatical. Sensible and down to earth – advice we would give to someone else who had run themselves into the ground, but which we find hard to apply to ourselves.

The second stage was Horeb: that is Mount Sinai, the mountain of God (1 Kgs. 19:8). That was where God had appeared to Moses and revealed his great name and

called him to lead his people out of Egypt. It was where
he had met with his people and with Moses and given
them his law and covenant. It was God's place, and God
wanted Elijah to remember that he was God, the God
who saves, and calls, and commands, and promises his
presence.

Here's another way God refreshes his people. He calls
us to turn away from focusing on ourselves, on our situation and problems, and to look instead at him. Take
time to focus on the big God, the one who is glorious and
sovereign and holy; the one who comes, and loves, and
speaks, and blesses, and so much more. With the
psalmists recall his wonderful deeds in the past;
immerse yourself again in the great truths of the Bible;
remember his faithfulness and his promises that he will
never fail or leave you.

Then God listened. He gave Elijah a chance to off
load – the third stage in the process of refreshing.
Twice he asked, 'What are you doing here, Elijah?' (1
Kgs. 19:9,13). It wasn't as though he didn't know; he
certainly didn't need Elijah to say the same thing all
over again. But Elijah needed to say it. Twice. He needed to talk it through. In fact he needed a good moan, to
get all the negatives churning inside him out into the
open so that God could deal with them. Talking
through how we feel or having a good moan isn't likely to solve all our problems overnight, but, rightly
done, it can be a significant step towards renewal and
refreshment.

Some find it easy to talk direct with God; others need
a wise Christian friend with whom they can talk things
through and then together take them to God in prayer.
Certainly God has given us friends to help us through
the tough times, and we're foolish if we try to carry the
burden all on our own. However you do it, pour out

your problems and needs; God wants to take them up and give you his refreshing.

The fourth stage in God's refreshing was a new encounter with himself. 'Go out and stand on the mountain in the presence of the LORD,' he said, 'for the LORD is about to pass by' (1 Kgs. 19:11). Well, we can guess what's coming. This is Sinai, where God showed his glory and his might to his people; at his presence the mountain shook, thunders roared, lightning flashed; cloud and fire and smoke, and the mighty voice of the mighty God. If the fire of God fell on Mount Carmel, how much more will it fall on Sinai!

But it didn't. A great and powerful wind, tearing the mountains apart and shattering the rocks – but God was not in the wind. Then an earthquake – but God was not in the earthquake. Then fire – but God was not in the fire. Then a still small whisper, the sound of gentle quietness. God knew that that was what Elijah needed; he needed his God. He'd had the fireworks on Carmel, and they were fine in their place. Moses and the Israelites had had the storm and the darkness. But what Elijah needed just at that time to refresh and renew him was quietness. 'When Elijah heard it, he pulled his cloak over his face and went out and stood at the mouth of the cave' (1 Kgs. 19:13).

When we need refreshing, the thing we need above all is God himself. It doesn't matter how he comes; we may need the thunder and the fire. Or we may need the sound of gentle quietness. Whatever way we need him God knows, and that's the way he'll come.

The next thing God did to refresh Elijah was to give him some facts and promises (1 Kgs. 19:15-18). The first was that God was still in charge; he knew what he was doing; he raised up kings and he cast them down, all in his good time. Elijah was not alone; God was giving him

Elisha to be with him and to succeed him as prophet. And in response to Elijah's warped understanding of the situation he said, 'I reserve seven thousand in Israel – all whose knees have not bowed to Baal and all whose mouths have not kissed him' (1 Kgs. 19:18). God didn't directly answer all the points Elijah had raised with him, but he told him enough to lift him up and give him hope.

The final stage of God's refreshing of Elijah was to give him work to do. Elijah was an activist, and God knew that. God knows you too, better than you know yourself. It may be that God will choose to refresh you by giving you a long time of idleness in which you can wait on him and renew your strength. Or he may give you a task and anoint you again with his Spirit, so you can know the joy and refreshing power of working for him. How he does it is up to him; what you have to do is allow him to do it, to show in your life that he is the God who refreshes.

Lord, here I am – dry, weary, hurt, afraid, depressed, struggling. I need you to refresh me and renew me. How you do it is up to you: through a miracle or through rest and medicines and caring friends. But do it, Lord; as you did it for Elijah, do it for me. For I am yours, and you are my God.

26.

Jeremiah and the God who calls

God has called you. He's the God who calls, and he hasn't missed you out. He's called you in the way he calls all his people: to follow Jesus, live a holy life, tell others about him, and so on. But he's also called you in specific ways, to tasks for which you are uniquely equipped. The possible range of tasks is huge, from being a parent to running a senior citizens' club, from being a missionary to using your financial skills to help a Christian charity. Over the past few weeks he's been calling me to a new project in a remote area of Wales; perhaps he has a specific task that he's about to set before you.

A call from God may be to a lifetime's ministry, or it may be to a task that takes a few days. It may be to something high profile for which you'll get recognition and praise; it may be to obscurity and pain and suffering. It may be to preach the gospel to thousands; it may be to be a witness for Jesus in a fireworks factory.

It could be that you're not aware of God's call. You've never heard a voice in the stillness of the night, or seen a vision on a Damascus road. What you do you do because you decided to do it, or because someone asked you to do it, not because God has called you to it. That's a shame; although what you're doing may be good, it is nowhere near as worthwhile as doing it because God has called you to do it. Of course, it's possible that God has called you to do it, but you're not aware of his call; but it would be so much more meaningful if you were able to face each task consciously aware that it's a task God has specifically given to you.

So, as we look at look at the way God called one individual, Jeremiah, listen for the call of God to you, perhaps confirming what you're already doing, or setting before you a new task. He is the God who calls; ask him to call you. After all, you've only one life to live on earth. You may as well make sure that you spend it doing the things he wants you to do.

1. *Formed, known, set apart and appointed.*

> The word of the LORD came to me, saying,
>> 'Before I formed you in the womb I knew you,
>> before you were born I set you apart;
>> I appointed you as a prophet to the nations.' (Jer. 1:4-5)

God had a purpose for Jeremiah. His parents and personality and circumstances and life weren't random chance things. Before he was born God was working to shape him for the task he wanted him to do. The same is true of each of us. God knows the tasks he has for us to do; from before we were born he's been shaping us, through all the different experiences we've had, both pleasant and unpleasant, to give us what it takes to do those tasks. Of course, the fact that God has shaped us for these tasks doesn't force us to do them; we're free to refuse his call and to waste the skills and experiences God has given us. But why be so foolish? Surely the purposes that God has for our lives are going to be the very best. There's a great verse later in Jeremiah, where God says, 'I know the plans I have for you…plans to prosper you and not to harm you, plans to give you hope and a future' (Jer. 29:11). They may not be the easiest or even the most obvious, but God's plans for each step of our lives have got to be good, far better than anything we can dream up.

2. *Wriggling*. 'Sorry, Lord, you've got it wrong. You've got the wrong man. For a job like that you need a good speaker, somebody with tons of experience and lots of clout. I'm just a kid; I won't do.' Jeremiah wasn't the first to wriggle at God's call. Moses did it very skilfully; Gideon had a good go at it. So have the rest of us. Maybe it is laziness, or fear, or inertia, or unbelief, or an automatically negative reaction when somebody tells us to do something. But it didn't get Jeremiah very far, nor Moses or Gideon, for that matter. 'As I was saying a moment ago, Jeremiah, I know all about you; I know everything there is to know about your age and your experience and your speaking abilities. And I'm still calling you.' So there it is. We may think up all sorts of excuses; some of them may be very ingenious and sound convincing. But they don't convince God, whose ingenuity is far greater than ours. There's an ironic touch to Jeremiah's wriggle in verse 6: he starts off, 'Ah, Sovereign LORD.' That is hardly a suitable introduction to telling God he's made a mistake. Either he's the sovereign Lord of our lives or he isn't. If he isn't, our Christian lives will be a disaster. If he is, we may as well not waste time arguing with him.

3. *'Don't be afraid.'* Jeremiah may have been young, but he wasn't daft. He knew that what God was calling

him to do would be tough. In his days it wasn't a problem being a prophet; there were lots of prophets telling the people what they wanted to hear. The problem was being a true prophet of the true God and telling the people his message, one that they most certainly didn't want to hear. Jeremiah was a sensitive man, easily hurt. If he obeyed God's call he knew he would get hurt; there would be times of darkness and desolation; he would suffer for his God. Yet twice God commands him not to hang back through fear (Jer. 1:8,17). You may be a fearless person who revels in God's call to a difficult and dangerous task; but most of us have to struggle with fears. What if I'm not hearing God properly? What if other people laugh at me? What if I'm not up to it? What if I try and fail? What if things turn out really tough? God's response is 'Don't let that stop you.' He doesn't tell us there's nothing to be afraid of; serving him is always tough; risks and potential pitfalls are always there. When he called Paul he bluntly stated, 'I will show him how much he must suffer for my name' (Acts 9:16). But he still calls us to set aside those fears, to get up on our feet and to do what he commands (Acts 9:17).

4. *The God who calls is always with us.* If he couldn't promise this he wouldn't call us. He knows even better than we do that we couldn't do the job without him. Let the tremendous truth 'I am with you' (Jer. 1:8,19) be the foundation of everything you do in response to his call. Do nothing on your own. Indeed, without him you can do nothing (Jn. 15:5). Through him you can do all things (Phil. 4:13). Make sure the work is his work, the ministry his ministry. Soak it in prayer; do everything in the name of Jesus and in the power of the Holy Spirit.

5. *Empowering.* 'Go into all the world and make disciples' said Jesus to his disciples; 'but don't go until
   you've received God's power,' the power that was to
   come at Pentecost. The God who calls us is with us;
   because he's with us his power is with us, and we can
   know that power working through our weakness,
   using us for his glory. God reached out his hand,
   touched Jeremiah's mouth, and said:

   > 'Now, I have put my words in your mouth. See, today I
   > appoint you over nations and kingdoms to uproot and
   > tear down, to destroy and overthrow, to build and to
   > plant....Today I have made you a fortified city, an iron
   > pillar and a bronze wall to stand against the whole land
   > – against the kings of Judah, its officials, its priests and
   > the people of the land. They will fight against you but
   > will not overcome you, for I am with you and will rescue
   > you.' (Jer. 1:9-10, 18-19)

6. *Keeping going.* Jeremiah obeyed God's call to be a prophet
   for at least forty years, but not without a struggle. Again
   and again he was tempted to give up; at times he cried
   out to God in despair and desolation. All through those
   forty years God continued to be with him and keep him,
   in fulfilment of his promise. But that didn't make life any
   easier. Indeed, things got tougher. On one celebrated
   occasion, when Jeremiah had cried out to God over an
   issue he was struggling with, God replied:

   > 'If you have raced with men on foot
   >   and they have worn you out,
   >   how can you compete with horses?
   > If you stumble in safe country,
   >   how will you mange in the thickets by the Jordan?
   >   (Jer. 12:5)

Hardly an encouraging response! 'Jeremiah,' says God, 'things are tough, and they're going to get tougher. What I'm asking you to do is to keep going.' Not all tasks last forty years. Nor does God insist we stick at every job he gives us until it's finished. Paul left many a church half planted and moved on to the next place after only a few weeks. God may call us to start a job, and then pass it on to someone else to complete. But whatever you do, don't give up the job when God is still calling you to keep at it. It may take longer than you anticipated. It will probably be tougher than you expected; you may get discouraged and feel you're making no progress. But don't give up – not until he tells you to. This means, of course, that you will need to be listening for his continuing call all the time you're serving him. The call to a task isn't just at the beginning; it continues right through until the end. So keep going back to him, to check that you're hearing him right, that you're going in the right direction, that you're still with him and he is still with you.

Lord, I want to do your thing. Please keep calling me and empowering me; give me the grace to hear and follow, even when it's tough. If it's a task I've been doing for a long time, renew my calling so I know you're with me in it. If it's a new task, give me courage and faith to go forward with you.

27.

Timothy and the God who equips

The God who calls is also the God who equips. Just as God called and equipped the young and fearful Jeremiah to be a prophet, so, more than six hundred years later, he called and equipped the young and fearful Timothy to serve him as a leader in his church. Timothy had an extensive ministry, travelling with Paul and ministering in many churches. We shall use the two letters that Paul wrote to encourage and instruct Timothy to illustrate some of the ways our God equips us for his work.

1. *God equips us with the gospel.* Every task that God calls us to do is part of his great purpose of salvation, of bringing good news to a lost world. As a result, in every situation, we go as 'Christ's ambassadors' (2 Cor. 5:20) showing by our lives and declaring by our words the great truths of the gospel of God's grace, and, supremely, bringing people face to face with the Lord Jesus. In each of his letters Paul reminds Timothy that he's been entrusted with the gospel; in

the face of 'godless chatter' and false teachings he must hold faithfully on to it and pass it on to others (1 Tim. 6:20-21; 2 Tim. 1:13-14). God doesn't send us into a hurting world simply with high hopes and good intentions. He sends us with his word, his message. It's a gospel that is 'the power of God for salvation for everyone who believes' (Rom. 1:16). It has the power to change lives, to set free captives, to push back the frontiers of the kingdom of darkness. Don't be ashamed of it, even if you suffer for it, Paul told Timothy; tell them the gospel; show them Jesus (2 Tim. 1:8).

2. *God equips us with the Bible*. This follows on closely from our first point, since it's to the Bible we turn to find the truths of the gospel. But Paul makes a specific point of reminding Timothy of the significance of the Scriptures for his service and ministry. After talking about the suffering that those who serve God will go through, and the deceits of 'evil men', Paul writes:

> But as for you, continue in what you have learned and have become convinced of, because you know those from whom you learned it, and how from infancy you have known the holy Scriptures, which are able to make you wise for salvation through faith in Christ Jesus. All Scripture is God-breathed and is useful for teaching, rebuking, correcting and training in righteousness, so that the man of God may be thoroughly equipped for every good work. (2 Tim. 3:14-17)

For Timothy, of course, 'Scriptures' would primarily have meant the Old Testament, but since Paul also refers to the gospel message that he had 'learned and…become convinced of' we're justified in using this passage to remind us of the value of the whole Bible. If you've got the Bible you've got what you need to equip you 'thoroughly' for every good work. Here are the truths on which we can build our lives; here are the promises that enable us to step out in faith as we follow and serve the Lord. Here are the answers to so many of life's puzzles. Here are instructions and commands for so many situations. Here is light that shines into the darkness. Here is the word of God that can answer the devil's lies. Get hold of the Bible; let it shape and empower you. Know it; use it; it's a key piece of equipment for every task that God will set before you.

3. *God equips us with his Holy Spirit.* Every Christian has the Holy Spirit, but it is God's purpose to equip us for specific tasks; that's the purpose of the gifts of the Spirit. They're not toys for us to play with, or status symbols to boost our egos. They're the way God enables us to do the work to which he calls us. If he calls us to teach then he gives us the gift of teaching. If he calls us to care for those who are in need he gives us the gift of mercy; if he calls us to exercise a ministry of healing, he gives us the gift of healing. Again, in each of his letters, Paul reminds Timothy of the Holy Spirit and the gifting he has given him:

> Do not neglect your gift, which was given you through a prophetic message when the body of elders laid their hands on you... I remind you to fan into flame the gift of God, which is in you through the laying on of my hands. For God did not give us a spirit of timidity, but a spirit of power, love and of self-discipline. (1 Tim. 4:14; 2 Tim. 1:6-7)

These passages don't specify what gift (or gifts) Timothy had, but they make it clear that it was something very significant for his ministry. In his case the gift was given through the laying on of hands, and confirmed through a prophetic message. Gifts can be given in many different ways, but prayer and the laying on of hands by the elders of a church are a special means God uses as we are set apart for a specific task – whether it's a new responsibility in the church, or starting a new job in our everyday life. Paul unpacks something of what having the gift of the Holy Spirit means by listing 'power', 'love' and 'self-discipline'. Each of these deserves a section to itself.

4. *God equips us with power.* This isn't power as understood in the secular world. It's not power to smash our enemies or to force people to believe. It's not pressure or manipulation or control. It's the kind of power Paul demonstrated at Corinth: 'I came to you in weakness and fear, and with much trembling. My message and my preaching were not with wise and persuasive words, but with a demonstration of the Spirit's power, so that your faith might not rest on men's wisdom, but on God's power' (1 Cor. 2:3-5). That's the power to get for whatever task God calls you to do.

5. *God equips us with love.* 'In my service for God' says Paul, 'I may do the most amazing things, but if I haven't got love I'm nothing and I achieve nothing.' Love, God's love poured into our hearts by the Holy Spirit (Rom. 5:5), is essential for any task we undertake in response to God's call. It may be that for some reason or another you don't find it easy to love some of the staff in the workplace, or some of the youngsters in

the youth group where you're a leader. For God that's not a problem; he knows that on our own there are some people we simply can't love. That's why he gives us the gift of love through the Holy Spirit, so that we can live love, do love and show love, even where we don't feel love. Ask God for all sorts of gifts of his Spirit, but ask him above all for the infilling of love (1 Cor. 12:31, 14:1).

6. *God equips us with a saved mind.* The AV translated the third thing that Paul says the Spirit gives us a 'sound mind.' More recent translations tend to have 'self-discipline', but that only gives part of the meaning of the word Paul uses, which is made up of two roots – one being the word from which the New Testament gets 'save', 'salvation' and 'Saviour' – and the other being a common word for our mind and heart. So Paul isn't just talking about the Spirit helping Timothy to hold in check those youthful passions to which he was subject (2 Tim. 2:22), but the Spirit permeating and 'saving' every area of his inner being, his thinking, his beliefs, his feeling, his willing and his desiring. This is the process of the 'renewing' of our minds that Paul writes about in Romans 12:2. It's not something that we can do by our own effort; it has to be the work of the Spirit in us. To fill us with 'the mind of Christ' (1 Cor. 2:16) is a vital way God equips us to serve and live for him.

7. *God equips us with each other.* In many ways the most significant piece of equipment God gave Timothy for his ministry was Paul. We're not sure if Paul was actually the means of Timothy's conversion, but Paul did take him under his wing when he was a young Christian and mentored and trained him. He gave

him opportunities to serve as Timothy joined his team on his missionary journeys. He watched over him, prayed for him, loved him, commended him to others, encouraged him, corrected him, wrote letters to him, and gave him the benefit of all his experience and wisdom. Many times Timothy must have thanked God for what he gave him in giving him Paul. Each of us, too, has benefited from the Christians God has put alongside us from time to time. They may be those who have taught us, or pastored us, or mentored us in some formal way; or they may be colleagues or friends who, without having a specific role in caring for us, have encouraged and supported us, loved us, prayed for us, set us a godly example and shown us Jesus. Such people are God's precious gift to us, and through them he shapes and equips us to be the people he wants us to be and to serve him in the places he has put us.

8. *God equips us with prayer.* When Paul wrote to Timothy he stated that night and day he continually remembered him in his prayers (2 Tim. 1:3). In his instructions about how things should be done in the church at Ephesus, the first thing he mentioned was prayer: 'I urge, then, first of all, that requests, prayers, intercession and thanksgiving be made for everyone... I want men everywhere to lift up holy hands in prayer' (1 Tim. 2:1,8). A key piece of equipment God gives us is prayer, both prayer for us by others, and prayer by us for ourselves and for those we are seeking to serve. Prayer not only opens the windows of God's blessing: bringing each aspect of our service regularly to God helps ensure that we're doing it in his strength and in his way, rather than going off on some tangent of our own.

Thank you Lord that you are the God who equips. Never again will I say 'I couldn't do that' when you call me to do something. If you ask me to do it, I'll do it, and look to you to give me what it takes. I know I can depend on you, and that if I go forward in faith you'll never let me down.

28.

Peter and the God who forgives

There's a hugely significant incident that took place on the day Jesus rose from the dead about which the New Testament is silent. The gospel writers describe for us how the risen Lord met the women and Mary Magdalene in the garden. They tell the story of Jesus meeting the two disciples on the road to Emmaus. They give two accounts of Jesus showing himself to those gathered in the upper room. But they are silent about what happened when Peter met Jesus.

All we know is that the risen Lord met with Peter some time between his visit to the empty tomb early in the morning of the first Easter Day and the evening of that day when the two disciples rushed back from Emmaus (Lk. 24:34; 1 Cor. 15:5). When that happened we don't know, nor where. Nor do we know what passed between them. It may well be that Peter never told anyone, so personal and so precious was that time they spent together.

If Peter never told anyone, then it's probably not right for us to probe and try to guess what happened. We know for sure that when Peter met his risen Lord he was a broken man, with all that he had lived for over the past three years in ruins. Worse still, on his soul lay the awful burden of his sin. Judas had sinned grievously in betraying Jesus with a kiss in the garden; was Peter's sin any less? He had vowed that he would stick by Jesus even if everyone else deserted him – and then in the courtyard of the high priest he called down curses on himself to convince the bystanders that he had nothing to do with him. Beyond doubt God had heard those curses. Beyond doubt he was now accursed. Judas had hanged himself; maybe Peter wished he had the courage to do the same.

In the upper room Jesus had spoken words that might have offered some hope: 'Simon, Simon, Satan has asked to sift you as wheat. But I have prayed for you, Simon, that your faith may not fail. And when you have turned back, strengthen your brothers' (Lk. 22:31). But how could he turn back? There was no-one to turn to; Jesus was dead.

Then came the message from Mary Magdalene that the tomb was empty. Peter frantically dashes with John through the empty streets to see. What they saw was enough to convince John, but Peter still struggled. Perhaps he dared not allow himself to hope for two incredible miracles: that Jesus should be alive, and that Jesus would forgive him. So he left the tomb and went back to where he was staying (Jn. 20:10).

When he did meet his Lord that Easter Day, did he turn and hide his face in shame? Was he afraid of the righteous judgment that Jesus must pronounce? Did he fall at his feet and beg for mercy? Or was he by then so numb with grief and horror that he had lost all feeling; did he just stand and gaze and wait?

We don't know. And we don't know what Jesus said to him. But we do know that the two incredible miracles happened: Jesus was alive, and Jesus did forgive him. He lifted from his soul that great weight of guilt and sin and failure. He washed Peter clean. He poured in healing and newness of life. He lifted him up; he renewed him in love; he flooded him with peace and hope and joy.

'Praise be to the God and Father of our Lord Jesus Christ!' Peter wrote at the start of his first letter. 'In his great mercy he has given us new birth into a living hope through the resurrection of Jesus Christ from the dead' (1 Pet. 1:3). 'Great mercy' – mercy great enough to forgive the greatest sin. 'Living hope' – in the power of that life and the joy of that hope Peter lived the rest of his life. And all of it 'through the resurrection of Jesus Christ from the dead', that greatest miracle of all.

Peter was by no means the only person in the Bible to know the miracle of God's forgiveness. There's no-one who didn't need it and no-one who asked for it and didn't receive it. Our God is the God who forgives.

- *God forgives – that's the gospel.* That's the message of the Bible. 'If you, O LORD, kept a record of sins, O LORD who could stand? But with you there is forgiveness; therefore you are feared' (Ps. 130:3-4). In Christ, says Paul, we have 'the forgiveness of sins, in accordance with the riches of God's grace that he lavished on us' (Eph. 1:7-8). That's what the cross is all about, Christ taking our sin, so that he could cry, 'Father, forgive them.' That's the message of the resurrection: sin's power broken, its captives set free.

- *God forgives – that's basic to our relationship with him.* When he forgives our sin he breaks down the barrier we have built between us and him. That means we can know him and his life in us. But if we build that barrier up again by continuing to sin and not letting him forgive us, we'll spoil that relationship. He'll not leave us all together; he'll still 'stand at the door and knock' (Rev. 3:20). But we won't have the glory and joy of having him in the centre of our lives.

- *God forgives – that's basic to our service for him.* Though we've no details of the meeting between Jesus and Peter on Easter Day, we've a full account of the meeting between them by the lakeside, when Jesus called and commissioned Peter afresh to the work he had for him. Two themes dominated the conversation: love and service. 'Simon, son of John, do you truly love me?... Feed my lambs' (Jn. 21:15). Both love and service went back to that Easter Day experience of forgiveness. Peter loved much because he'd been forgiven much (Lk. 7:47); he had to be a forgiven man to be the man God was going to use to care for his people. We have to allow God to make us clean for him to use us. 'If I had cherished sin in my heart,' said the psalmist, 'the LORD would not have listened' (Ps. 66:18). If I have unforgiven sin in my life my service for God will be ineffective.

- *God forgives – but we can decline to be forgiven.* God offers forgiveness, but he doesn't force us to receive it. We may choose to prefer our sin to him. We may refuse to turn from it and turn to him. We may erect a barrier between us and his forgiveness by hanging on to an unforgiving spirit towards someone else (Mt. 6:15).

- *God forgives – again and again.* In the Lord's Prayer the request for forgiveness follows the request for daily bread. Our need of forgiveness is as regular as our need for food. God's supply of forgiveness never runs out; he tells us to keep coming back to him for more. Even if we've committed the same sin many times before, even if we'd vowed we'd never do it again, he is the God who forgives. This doesn't mean, of course, that we can treat sin lightly, or play on God's grace. Every time we come to him for forgiveness we acknowledge how 'utterly sinful' sin is, and we consciously turn our back on it, recognizing that we have 'died' to it and are committed to live in it no longer (Rom. 7:13, 6:1-2).

- *God forgives – all our sins.* Big sins, little sins. Sins we're ashamed of, and sins we enjoy. Open sins, secret sins. One offs, and sins we do again and again. Sins listed in the Bible and sins the Bible doesn't mention. Sins we're conscious of, and sins we don't even realize we've committed. None of them are too hard for him, provided we let him forgive them. The only unforgivable sin is refusing to let the Holy Spirit bring us to him for forgiveness, so hardening our heart that we won't let the Spirit of God do anything with us. The stern warning of Jesus to the Pharisees in Matthew 12:31-32 doesn't mean that if we resist the work of the Spirit for a time or say something against him or even use his name as a swear word we have committed an unforgivable sin. He will forgive us even these things if we turn to him in repentance. What Jesus was warning the Pharisees against was reaching the point in their rejection of him and of the work of the Spirit where their hearts were so hard that they could not repent, and so could not be forgiven. The best known Pharisee, who undoubtedly hardened his heart for years against Jesus and the Holy Spirit, found that there was forgiveness even for him, 'the worst of sinners' (1 Tim. 1:15-16).

- *God forgives – and that's a fact.* Sometimes we have problems over forgiveness because we don't feel forgiven. We've repented, turning from our sin; we've asked God to forgive; but we don't feel any different. Since we tend to be controlled by our feelings, we then begin to think that we've not really been forgiven. But God's forgiveness is a fact, not a feeling. Just as his love is constant, whether we feel it or not, so his forgiveness is certain, whether we feel forgiven or not. Part of our problem is that though God is so ready to forgive and forgives so completely, we tend to hang on to our feelings of guilt and shame and find it difficult to forgive ourselves. Naturally enough, if we continue to hold on to such things they will affect our feelings; what we need to do is give them over to God too, and let him sort them out.

- *God forgives – and gives us a ministry of forgiveness.* The phrase about forgiveness in the Lord's Prayer makes it clear that if we belong to a forgiving God then we will be forgiving people. What he's done for us we'll do for others. Sometimes we find it very hard, and in some situations it may be a matter of praying, 'Lord I forgive; help my unforgiveness.' Those whose loved ones have been brutally killed by a terrorist bomb, or who were systematically abused when they were children may find anger and bitterness rising up in them again and again. What God looks for is not that we never feel hurt by sins that others have committed against us. Rather, it is a willingness to be brought to the point where we can forgive. The thing that God can't forgive would be a fixed attitude: 'I will not forgive. I'm determined never to forgive. I will nurse my hatred and anger for the rest of my life.' In addition to calling us to forgive others, God sends us into his world with a message of forgiveness: the proclamation to everyone that his way is the way of forgiveness, and that he is the God who will receive and welcome all who turn from their sin to him, the God who forgives.

What a God: the God who forgives! I praise you, Lord; I marvel at your grace; I rejoice at your forgiveness made possible by the death and resurrection of Jesus. Lord, whose forgiveness was big enough for Peter, forgive me too all my sins. Set me free from their power; deal with anything that would spoil my relationship with you, and draw me close to your heart.

29.

David and the faithful God

Everyone who walks with God finds him faithful. His character is consistent; his love and grace and holiness are constant. His truth is dependable; if he says something we can trust it; if he makes a promise he will keep it. His commitment to us is unchanging – we may come and go in our feelings towards him, we may wander away and do our own thing, we may neglect him or forget him – but he never fails us or leaves us.

David used a great phrase in one of his psalms:

> Your love, O LORD, reaches to the heavens,
>   your faithfulness to the skies. (Ps. 36:5)

We'll use David's best-known Psalm to help unpack something of the greatness of God's faithfulness that he experienced in any number of ways throughout his life.

1. *The faithful LORD.* When we read the words of Jesus, 'I am the good shepherd' (Jn. 10:11) we tend to rush over the 'I am' to get to the 'good shepherd.' That is a mistake. When Jesus spoke those words he put special stress on the 'I am.' Indeed, in effect, he was saying

I AM, taking upon himself the great name of God given to Moses in Exodus 3:14, 'I AM WHO I AM.' It wasn't so much, 'Here before you you see the good shepherd.' Rather it was 'The good shepherd you see before you is nothing less than the great God, the I AM.' The same is true of the opening words of Psalm 23, 'The LORD is my shepherd.' 'The one who cares for me,' David is saying, 'is none other than the great LORD, the I AM, the one who revealed his name to Moses and has shown his faithfulness all down the years: the mighty God, the Living God, the sovereign God.' There's no-one like the God of Israel, declared Moses, who rides on the heavens to help his people, and on the clouds in his majesty; 'the eternal God is our refuge, underneath us are the everlasting arms' (Deut. 33:26-27). That's our God; he's big; we can trust him to be faithful.

2. *The faithful shepherd.* Sheep are vulnerable. Left to their own devices they wouldn't last long. They need a shepherd to care for them. Some shepherds are good; some are bad. Some can be trusted; some can't. Some neglect the sheep and look after their own interests; some run away when they see the wolf coming (Ezek. 34:1-16; Jn. 10:11-16). Not so our God. He is the faithful shepherd, the one who really cares, the one we can trust at all times.

3. *The faithful provider.* A key role of the shepherd in Bible times was to make sure the sheep were fed and watered. In dry seasons and desert areas finding food and drink was no easy task; if the shepherd failed them the sheep would die. So when David writes that God 'makes me lie down in green pastures, he leads me besides quiet waters' (Ps. 23:2) he's not telling us that his God always gives him an easy life. Rather,

he's unpacking the second part of verse 1, 'I shall not be in want.' Our God knows what we need. He knows what we need materially; he knows what we need emotionally; he knows what we need spiritually. What's more, he has the resources to supply all those needs, and he's committed himself to do so. 'My God will meet all your need according to his glorious riches in Christ Jesus' (Phil. 4:19). So we don't have to be anxious, running around stressed and worried like the 'pagans' who don't have a Heavenly Father (Mt. 6:25-34). We have a faithful God, who knows what we need and who will always provide it.

4. *The faithful potter.* God's provision reaches into all areas of our lives, and especially into that part of our lives we might call our soul. The phrase David uses is a broad one: 'he restores my soul' (Ps. 23:3). It could be translated in all sorts of ways, including 'he refreshes my whole being', 'he gives me back my life', 'he renews my spirit', 'he gives me second wind', 'he restores my relationship with him', 'he renews my strength', 'he gives me a new beginning', 'he revives my life', and 'he gives me new life.' For me it speaks of the way God is working on me; the Master Potter reshaping the spoilt pot, making me into something beautiful (Jer. 18:3-4). Being shaped by God can be a painful process, and it is one that we rarely understand. But he's committed to doing it, to making us like Jesus, conforming us to 'the likeness of his Son', transforming us 'into his likeness with ever increasing glory' (Rom. 8:29; 2 Cor. 3:18). What he's doing is wise and good, and we can trust him to do it well.

5. *The faithful guide.* 'He guides me in paths of righteousness for his name's sake' (Ps. 23:3). I certainly

need his guidance. I have decisions to make, problems to face, a life to live. Left on my own I would soon make a mess of things. So I need a guide I can trust, someone who knows the right way, and who will faithfully lead me in it. I used to think that decision making would grow easier as I grew older, but it hasn't done so. Life seems more complex than ever, and the issues never seem to be straightforward. Often I've had to pray, 'Lord, I believe this is the right way forward, and it's the way I'm going. But if I've got it wrong please show me or stop me.' But looking back I can without a question see the way God has kept his hand upon me and guided me faithfully in his paths.

6. *Faithful in the valley.* David knew full well that having the LORD as his shepherd and provider, the restorer of his soul and his guide, didn't mean that everything in life would be easy. Psalm 23 now turns to the shadow side, to the valley (Ps. 23:4). David knew what it was to be in the dark valley; he knew opposition and setbacks, suffering and pain, death and bereavement. He also knew sin and failure, and the 'rod' of God chastening and correcting him. Like the rest of us he was familiar with the dark times of life, yet he could say, 'I fear no evil, for you are with me.' His God was faithful; he stuck with him when things were tough. Even when he uttered that great cry in the awful darkness of the previous psalm, 'My God, my God, why have you forsaken me?' (Ps. 22:1) God was still there. Even when he sinned with Bathsheba, his God did not forsake him. It's good to have a God who is faithful when you're on the mountain tops; it's even better to have a God who is faithful in the darkness of the valleys.

7. *Extra faithful when the enemy's around.* Many times I've heard people say that wherever the Lord is at work, the devil will soon get to work too. Doubtless there's truth in that, but Psalm 23:5 gives us the reverse truth: whenever the enemy's around, God's around. And he's not just hanging around doing nothing. He's hard at work laying out a feast. That's a promise to remember next time the devil is having a really good go at you, or, indeed, when those who are fighting against you because you belong to God are particularly active: even if you don't see him, God is there, spreading before you a rich banquet which is yours to enjoy. That's our faithful God.

8. *Faithful in the good times.* The next two phrases, 'You anoint my head with oil; my cup overflows' (Ps. 23:5) may still be describing God's faithfulness when our enemies are around. But we'll use them to remind us that God is faithful in the good times as well as in the bad. Anointing with oil symbolizes many things: care for a guest; honour for a VIP; cooling and soothing; cleansing and healing; joy and beauty. Additionally, priests and kings were anointed when they were set apart for service, symbolizing the holiness and presence of God with them. Supremely, for us, anointing speaks of the Holy Spirit. 'Christ' means anointed. At the start of his ministry Jesus applied to himself the words of Isaiah, 'The Spirit of the Sovereign LORD is upon me, because the LORD has anointed me to preach good news to the poor' (Is. 61:1). That same Spirit who anointed Jesus is freely available for each one of us. We too have the privilege of being anointed by none other than the Sovereign LORD himself. The picture of the overflowing cup reminds us further of God's generosity and abundance; he's more

willing to give than we are to receive; he gives even
more than we can take. Not all of life is dark valleys;
in the times of blessing and rejoicing God continues
to show his overflowing faithfulness.

9. *Faithful all the days of our lives.*

> Surely goodness and love will follow me
>   all the days of my life,
> and I will dwell in the house of the LORD
>   for ever. (Ps. 23:6)

There's an interesting feel to the word David uses for
'follow' here. It pictures goodness and love pursuing
us, chasing along behind us like hounds on our trail.
There's something tenacious about the word.
Goodness and love aren't casually happening to come
along behind us. Like the hound of heaven, they
never give up on us, never let us out of their sight.
The word David uses here for love, too, speaks of
God's faithfulness; it is his unfailing loyal covenant
love, to which he has committed himself, and from
which he will never turn. God's goodness, God's
unfailing faithful love will dog our steps every inch of
the way every day of our lives.

*Yes, Lord, that's what I need: your faithfulness and
goodness and love all the days of my life. And I
know it's what you give. Thank you, Lord. Like
David I trust you, I put everything I am and do
and have to face into the hands of my faithful God.
You will never fail me or forsake me, faithful God.*

Emmanuel the God who is with us

Some trust in chariots and some in horses,
  but we trust in the name of the LORD our God. (Ps. 20:7)

Hebrew is a very succinct language, but it packs a lot of meaning into a small space. This verse is twice as long in English as it is in Hebrew, and even then there's still more meaning we can unpack.

'These guys here are chariot people,' says David 'and those guys over there are horse people.' You can picture them. That one's just bought a new chariot. He's parked it outside his house. He's polished it up, even though it's just come from the showroom. Soon he'll be driving it around, watching for people to notice it and admire it and think what a clever guy he is to have it. When you talk to him it's all chariot: design, gadgets, speed, comfort, the latest model. He lives for his chariot: chariot is his life. Then there are the horse people. They live for horses; horses are their life. In the twenty-first century there are plenty of other things we can add to the list of what people live for, from football to family, from success to sex, from possessions to pleasure.

But we – and David specially underlines 'we' in contrast to the chariot and horse people – we are different. Our lives don't centre around chariots or horses or any of the other things. Maybe we have them, but they're not that important. We possess them, but they don't possess us. For us there's only one thing that matters, and that's the name of the LORD our God.

What do we do with the name of the LORD our God? The word David uses means basically to remember or call to mind. The NIV translates it 'trust'; other translators use 'make mention of', 'boast in' and 'pride ourselves on.' They're all trying to express the feel of the word: whatever other people may build their lives on, whatever else may fill their horizons, whatever they may put their trust in, for us it's the name of the LORD our God. That's what we fill our minds with. That's the basis of all our beliefs. That's what we live for. That's what we judge everything else by. That's what makes us what we are. That's our strength, our pride, our joy.

'The name', of course, is much more than a title. It covers all that God is: his character, his personality, his attributes, his nature. To build our lives on the name of the LORD our God means to take all the aspects of God that we've been looking at in this book, and all the other ones we've missed out, and to make them the basis of everything we are, the heart of our being, the foundation and motivation and inspiration of our thinking and living.

And the secret of that is Emmanuel. In no way can I by myself build my life on what God is. For a start my understanding of what he is and what it means to build my life on him is limited. More importantly, I haven't got what it takes to do it. So it's got to be him: Emmanuel, God with us. God living in us. God, the Father, the Son and the Holy Spirit, making his home in me and you, filling us with his fullness, renewing our mind, remoulding our character, shaping, changing, healing, empowering, and day by day living his life in us.

This is something big. This isn't just religion, or run-of-the-mill Christianity. This is God himself, the big God, the amazing fantastic holy powerful glorious God living in us and bringing all that he is, all his fullness, into our lives. If it wasn't there in the Bible we would say that it would be impossible, and far too good to be true. But it's there. It's God's promise, it's Emmanuel.

So how are you doing? How much of this big God have you got? How much of his nature? How much of his fullness? Or, much more importantly, how much do you want? Are you content with a bit? Are you drawing up limits, accepting this aspect of him but not that, letting him do a bit here but not there? Is he still having to knock on the door and ask to come in? Here's a checklist for you to work through, picking up some of the things that God has been saying to us as we've explored something of what he is, something of what it means to have the big God in our lives.

- *How hungry am I for God?* How much time do I spend seeking his face? Am I content with what I know and experience of him? What price would I pay to know him more?

- *Can I pray, 'Lord, show me your glory?'* Am I afraid of the glory of the Lord? Am I hungry for it? Can I say, 'To God be the glory' when it means I get no glory? Am I willing to let him show me his glory in any way he chooses?

- *Is my God the living God?* Is the world so real to me that God is unreal? If so, what am I going to do about it? Does God live in me? What difference does it make? How does it affect my thoughts, my actions, my hopes and fears? How is God changing my life? In what areas has he changed me over the past couple of years? Are there any bits of me that I'm not letting him touch? Are there any parts of me where I particularly need to say, 'Come, Lord, and change me here'?

- *How big is my God?* How can I 'magnify' him? Do I really accept that he's the creator of everything, including me? How does that affect the way I view the world around me? How fantastic is my God? Do I limit him to what I can understand? Would I still think him fantastic if he let me go through what Job went through? Can I cope with the mystery of God? What could I do to develop a greater sense of awe and wonder before him?

- *Do I really believe that God rules planet earth?* How could I increase the impact of that belief on the way I see world events? And what about my life – is he sovereign there? Is he big enough to be trusted when everything seems to be going wrong?

- *Have I really taken on board the call of God, 'Be holy because I am holy'?* Have I truly encountered the holiness of God? Am I willing to open my life up to it?

- *Do I call God 'Abba'?* If not, why not, and what could I do about it?

- *Do I put limits on the care and compassion and love of God?* What could I do to help me grasp 'how wide and long and high and deep' that love is? Where do I need to experience his love? And where do I need to learn to express it more?

- *Am I aware that God has come to me?* Have I welcomed him in, or is he still standing at the door knocking? Is he at home in my life? Am I filled with the Spirit? What areas still need to be filled with his fullness?

- *When did God last speak to me?* What did he say? Have I acted on what he said? How can I become better at hearing his voice? What is he saying to me at this moment?

- *Do I feel concerned about those who don't know Jesus?* How many people have I shared the good news with in this past year? Which of my neighbours or work colleagues need to hear the gospel? What am I going to do about it? How can I make sure that my life 'blesses' others?

- *Where have I experienced the power of God in my life?* Where have I seen it at work in the lives of others? How might I better grasp how great it is? Is his power 'at work within me'? Am I 'strong in the Lord and in his mighty power'? Am I happy with my weakness because God's power is 'being made perfect' in it?

- *Do I trust God's wisdom even when it looks like foolishness?*

- *Do I limit the grace of God, either towards me or towards others?* Can I thank God for the hurts he has allowed in my life? If not, what do I need to do?

- *Am I at a low in my Christian life?* If so, what steps could I take to help myself? What should I be asking God to do?

- *Am I aware of God's call?* Has he called me to my current job or situation? Is there something he's called me to do that I still haven't done? Is he calling me now to some specific task? How can I make sure I'm ready to hear his call when it comes? Do I trust him that when he calls he equips? Am I doing all I should to tap into his resources for the tasks I'm doing at the moment?

- *Have I received God's forgiveness for all my sin?* Am I living that forgiveness? Have I forgiven others? Have I forgiven myself?

- *Is my God trustworthy?* Do I trust his faithfulness, in the good times and in the bad times? Am I letting him shape me? Am I letting him guide me?

- *What am I building my life on?* What shapes my thinking? What motivates me? What controls my words and actions? Am I willing that 'the name of the Lord our God' should be the basis of all I am and do?

- *Am I ready and hungry to meet God, the real God, the big God?*

God, great God, my God.